This book belongs to:

_____

SYME'S LETTER WRITER

SYME'S LETTER WRITER

A GUIDE TO MODERN CORRESPONDENCE ABOUT (ALMOST) EVERY IMAGINABLE
SUBJECT OF DAILY LIFE, WITH ODES TO DESKTOP EPHEMERA, SELECTED
LETTERS OF FAMOUS WRITERS, EPISTOLARY RELATIONSHIPS,
FOUNTAIN PENS, TYPEWRITERS, STAMPS, STATIONERY,
AND EVERYTHING YOU NEED TO EMBARK
UPON ADVENTURES THROUGH
THE MAIL

RACHEL SYME

with illustrations from Joana Avillez

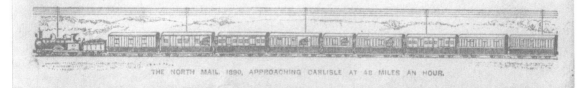

THE NORTH MAIL 1890, APPROACHING CARLISLE AT 48 MILES AN HOUR.

CLARKSON POTTER/PUBLISHERS
NEW YORK

Contents

USE ZIP CODE

Introduction

A LETTER FROM RACHEL

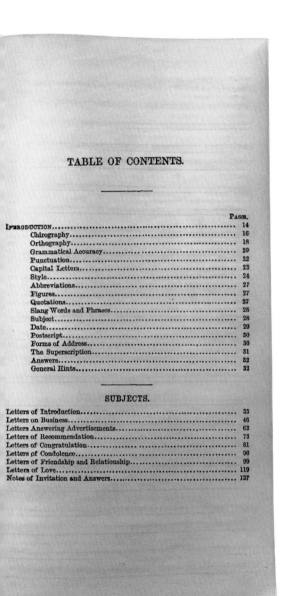

TABLE OF CONTENTS.

SUBJECTS.

I came across a copy of *Frost's Original Letter-Writer* online in the summer of 2020, when I had just started to write a lot of letters to strangers on my hideous, beige beater of an electric typewriter from the 1980s (she is a Nakajima AE-710 and I love her very much, and you will learn more about why in the Typewriters section later in this book; see page 162). I was on the hunt for the history of letter-writing, and my explorations led me down a rabbit hole that ended in Frost's guide, one of the first books to formally lay out tips and tricks of the mail-sending trade.

Frost's suggestions are hilariously outdated (I don't imagine many people today using her form letter for "answering an advertisement for a chambermaid"), but some of her wisdom holds up, such as her advice that using quotations or song lyrics in a letter feels twee and cheap ("Quotations should be used as a very rare luxury, as they are apt to give an appearance of pedantry and studied effect") or her choice of writing instruments: "Never write in pencil. It is always careless, often rude." Also, if you want to know how to send a truly creepy request to your fiancée asking for a lock of her hair while calling her a "stingy little pet," well, Frost has that covered too.

I share with you the story of S. A. Frost (and my favorite excerpt is on the next page—a truly deranged and bitchy form letter in which a man advises a younger acquaintance to ditch a friend) to say that, for as long as people have been flinging paper back and forth through the postal service, they have been wondering if they are doing it right.

Cottage industries have sprung up like barnacles in Frost's wake, offering suggestions for how best to open a letter (Is it *Dear*? Do people even say *dear* anymore?) and how to close one (Is *XOXO* too *Gossip Girl*? Does *Warmly* seem too tryhard or just tryhard enough? Would writing "All best" mark me as a sociopath?). Letters are such an intimate medium; they are meant for an audience of one. But, also, that one person will be spending a lot of time with whatever you send, poring over it with a hot beverage (or a cold cocktail) in hand. It makes sense that there is such public hand-wringing about such a private form. You want your letter to arrive at its destination, sure, but you also want it to really *arrive.* You want it to land. So people like Sarah Frost rush in to fill the void and to comfort the shaking hand over the blank page, ensuring nervous nellies that even a lackluster letter in the post is better than no letter at all.

I am, I admit, no Sarah Annie Frost-Shields. I have no hard-and-fast correspondence rules for you. I barely have any rules at all, except that you should apply the proper postage to your letters and learn how and when to use non-machinable stamps (and you will! See On Stamps on page 182). But this book is intended to be a nouveau *Frost's Original Letter-Writer* of sorts, one that takes Frost's boundless energy for telling confused people what to do and updates it for the modern—and decidedly not letter-centric—era. If Frost were alive today, she'd probably have a very popular TikTok account or a correspondence-themed Substack (her book *The Art of Dressing Well* does seem #cottagecore adjacent). But I have the pages of this book to work with, and I hope to provide a bit of structure around what I've learned when it comes to writing letters from the time I've spent on the PenPalooza project—a letter-exchange I launched on a whim during the early days of the pandemic that swelled to more than fifteen thousand members—and also from reading the correspondence of writers of the past. Like any good nineteenth-century prig, Sarah Frost did not trust anyone's opinion but her own. I don't possess so staunch an attitude. I have looked to other authors and poets and cooks and explorers and wanderers and the letters they have sent to inform my own how-tos—this is more of a group hymnal than a solo expedition.

LETTERS OF ADVICE.

LETTERS of Advice should never be written except by request. Even when they are most earnestly solicited they are very apt to prove disagreeable, and in many instances will give offence, even when written with the best motives.

Perfect frankness is an important requisite, as sincerity and singleness of purpose will often carry their own conviction.

Never offer advice after a folly or crime has been committed. It is worse than useless. You may give sympathy or reproof if it will benefit, but to point out the preventives after it is too late to use them is only wasting time, unless they are to prevent a repetition of the error.

In giving an opinion, be careful that you do not endeavor to make it a law, and do not be easily offended if your advice is disregarded. Your friend may have many counsellors beside yourself, or circumstances unknown to you may guide his course.

Above all, let no selfishness ever creep into a letter of advice. Put your friend's welfare and interest alone in the balance, or if it is a great scheme, the good of others, and let your advice be purely disinterested.

Use such letters judiciously and sparingly.

Advising a Young Man to Study a Profession.

COLUMBIA, May 23d, 18—.

DEAR ARCHIE,—Your letter announcing your sudden change of fortune, and asking my advice in regard to finishing your law studies, has just reached me. You say that your unexpected legacy will place you above the necessity of earning a support, and seem to consider it time wasted to still study for admission to the bar.

My dear boy, my advice to you would be to continue your studies

sfaction with his conduct and ability. He is a good workman, skil-
ul and rapid, having practised thoroughly all the higher branches
f his trade. I have found him reliable, honest and trustworthy,
nd he bears with him my warmest good wishes for future success
n business.

MARK MABERLEY.

Recommending a Farm Laborer.

Mr. ELI H. PRATT:

DEAR SIR,—In answer to your inquiries, I would state that the
earer, Perry Campbell, is thoroughly competent to discharge such
uties as you require. He has been for ten years on my farm, and
as a thorough knowledge of farm work of every description, is accus.
omed to the care of horses, cows and other animals, and I should
ave no hesitation in placing him in entire charge of a farm.

Very truly your's,
MARCUS WALTERS.

Declining to Recommend a Cook.

MEDIA, Dec. 8th, 18—.

Mrs. Watkins is surprised that Mary Malone should have had the
ssurance to refer to her, as she left her service for drunkenness and
nsolence.

Declining to Recommend a Clerk.

CHAMBERSBURG, Feb. 14th, 18—.

SIMON P. ALDEN Esq.:

SIR,—I regret that I cannot conscientiously write the testimonial
ou request of me. You are fully aware of the misconduct that
aused your discharge from my service, and it would be doing a
gross injustice for me to speak favorably to another employer. I
think an honest confession with a desire to reform, would be your
best recommendation.

Regretting that it is entirely out of my power to grant your request,

I am, in spite of your error,
Your sincere well wisher,
CYRUS KING.

The how-tos sprinkled throughout this book—How to Write a Postcard, How to Develop a Style in Your Correspondence, How to Write a Letter about Your Dreams, etc.—are meant as cheeky riffs on Frost's formatting, but are far less rigid (you won't find how to write a "Note Accompanying a Bouquet of Flowers to a Lady" here, or guidelines for a "Letter Recommending a Man Servant."). Instead, they are merely intended to get you writing and to make you excited to sit down and compose a letter. We'll explore how to write about a sumptuous meal, how to write a bitchy dispatch full of gossip and intrigue, and how to write about a beautiful spring day in a way that doesn't just feel like snoozy small talk. Along the way, there will be writing prompts, excerpts from letters past, lists of truly good, not overly pretentious $10 words to drop into your prose, care package suggestions, and tips on how to properly scent a perfumed letter. You will also find my version of a field guide to all the tangible, physical, touchable, collectible, snacky things you can use to liven up a letter. Fountain pens! Stamps! Embossing guns! Types of envelopes (yes, it gets wild . . .)!

In the bygone days when letters were the only way to communicate from afar, writing out a long, meandering note and tucking it into a plain envelope was more than enough to deliver a thrill. Everyone was *so bored!* Offering someone ten pages of scratchy handwriting that took the entire afternoon to read and broke up the monotony of the day? A *gift*. When you see people squeal and rush to the door in period films when the Pony Express arrives, they are not necessarily over-acting; receiving a piece of mail was perhaps the most exciting and exotic thing to happen to a person all week, maybe all month. Now, letters can barely compete with every other bit of stimulation flying at our faces, not because they have ceased to be thrilling, but because they have, for the most part, ceased to be at all.

There are so many reasons *not* to send a letter—it takes too long, it's unreliable, it requires scrounging up a stamp and a working pen, it might result in a hand cramp, it feels antiquated and unnatural and contrived. It's so much easier and more efficient to just pick up the phone or send a text. But letters still serve a vital purpose, which is that they exist to mock the very idea of efficiency. They require slow, gear-crunching effort on both ends, for the writer *and* for the reader (and for the many hands responsible for transporting the envelope in between the two). Letter-writing is a time-consuming rebuke to a world that tries to optimize every activity into a seamless slipstream, and there is joy to be had once you fully embrace the medium's outdated extravagance. If you are going to put in the work to send a piece of mail, why not stuff the envelope so full of little treasures that you re-enchant the recipient to the surprising possibilities of the form?

The truth is, nobody *has* to write letters anymore. We are all hilariously reachable, and yet, the last place anyone thinks to find us is inside our mailboxes. Snail mail's reputation has become that of an intrusive, junky nuisance at worst, and at best, a cringey affectation for people who think they are Jane Austen. But what if . . . we just decided to do it anyway? That is what I did, and it has brought me more joy, surprises, revelation, intimacy, and creativity than nearly anything else in my life over the past few years. This book is my attempt to pass those benefits along to you—and to push you past your inertia. Rummage through these pages. Read them out of order. Unlike Frost, I am not here to scold. I just want you to connect to someone else out there, late at night, scribbling away by candlelight. It's not the worst thing you can do with an extra hour. It might make someone's week, or month, or year. You have to send letters to receive letters. And you can start today.

DICTIONARY OF SYNONYMS.

ABANDON, *to*—desert, forsake, relinquish, renounce.
ABANDONED—corrupt, depraved, forsaken, profligate, reprobate, wicked.
ABASE, *to*—degrade, depress, disgrace, humble.
ABATE, *to*—decrease, diminish, lower, reduce, subside.
ABBREVIATE, *to*—abridge, curtail, condense, compress, epitomize, reduce, shorten.
ABET, *to*—connive, encourage, help.
ABHOR, *to*—abominate, detest, hate, loathe.
ABILITY — capacity, power, skill, strength, talent.
ABJURE, *to* — abnegate, recant, renounce, revoke.
ABLE—capable, clever, efficient, powerful, skilful, strong.
ABODE — dwelling, habitation, residence.
ABOLISH, *to*—abrogate, annul, destroy.
ABOMINATE, *to*—abhor, detest, hate.
ABRIDGE, *to*—contract, diminish, shorten.
ABSENT—abstracted, inattentive.
ABSOLUTE — arbitrary, positive, despotic, peremptory, unlimited.
ABSOLVE, *to*—acquit, clear, forgive, pardon, remit, set free.
ABSORB, *to*—engross, engulph, consume, imbibe, swallow up.
ABSTAIN, *to*—forbear, refrain.
ABSTRUSE—hidden, obscure.
ABSURD — foolish, irrational, ridiculous, preposterous.
ABUNDANT—ample, copious, plentiful, exuberant, plenteous.
ABUSIVE—insolent, insulting, offensive, opprobrious, reproachful, scurrilous.
ACCEDE, *to*—acquiesce, agree, consent, assent, comply, yield.
ACCEPT, *to*—admit, receive, take.
ACCEPTABLE — agreeable, grateful, welcome.

ACCESSION—addition, coming to, increase, augmentation.
ACCESSORY—abettor, accomplice, ally, assistant, associate.
ACCIDENTAL—casual, contingent, fortuitous, incidental.
ACCOMMODATE, *to*—adapt, adjust, fit, suit, serve.
ACCOMPLICE—abettor, accessory, ally, assistant, associate.
ACCOMPLISH, *to*—achieve, complete, effect, execute, fulfill, realize.
ACCOUNT—description, detail, explanation, narrative, narration, recital, relation.
ACCUMULATE, *to*—amass, gather, collect, heap up.
ACCURATE — correct, exact, precise, nice.
ACCUSE, *to* — arraign, censure, impeach; asperse, calumniate, defame, detract, vilify.
ACHIEVE, *to*—accomplish, effect, execute, complete, fulfill, realize.
ACERBITY—severity of temper, sour taste.
ACKNOWLEDGMENT — gratitude, concession.
ACKNOWLEDGE, *to* — avow, confess, grant, own, recognize.
ACQUAINT, *to*—apprise, communicate, disclose, inform, make known.
ACQUIESCE, *to*—accede, agree, assent, comply, consent, yield.
ACQUIRE, *to*—attain, earn, gain, obtain, procure, win.
ACQUIREMENT—acquisition, qualification.
ACQUIT, *to*—absolve, clear, forgive, pardon, set free.
ACQUITTANCE—deliverance, release.
ACRIMONY—harshness, smartness, asperity, tartness.
ACTIVE—agile, assiduous, industrious, alert, brisk, busy, lively, nimble, prompt, quick, vigorous.
ACTUAL—certain, genuine, positive, real.

67

From a Gentleman to a Lady Requesting an Explanation of Unfavorable Comments upon him.

WATER ST., Feb. 22d, 18—.

MISS OCTAVIA KNOW,—I have just had a long interview with a mutual friend of your's and mine, who has surprised me by repeating your unfounded assertions with regard to me. Of course, what is merely your opinion, I have no right to resent, though I regret that it should be so unfavorable, but I have a right to demand your grounds for asserting that I am an arrant flirt, a hypocrite, and concerned in more than one dishonorable transaction.

Will you have the kindness to inform me with whom I have flirted, how played the hypocrite, and in what dishonorable transactions I have been concerned.

OWEN FOLEVELL.

Reply to the Foregoing.

LA ROCHE ST., Feb. 22d, 18—.

OWEN FOLEVELL, ESQ.,—The high tone of your letter might impose upon one who was not so well acquainted with your history previous to your arrival at this place as I happen to be. My opinion was founded upon a knowledge of your life while you resided in St. Louis.

When I inform you that Mrs. Carrie Ryder is one of my most intimate friends and constant correspondent, you will not again request a list of your misdoings. If you consider your course of conduct in deceiving your uncle, endeavoring to ruin your young cousin Charles, and attempting to elope with an heiress of fifteen, honorable, I can only say that I differ in opinion.

OCTAVIA KNOW.

From a Gentleman to a Lady Remonstrating with her for Flirting.

No. 60 M—— ST., July 19th, 18—.

DEAR WINNIE,—You have promised one day to be my wife, and while accepting the entire devotion of my heart, have led me to suppose that you gave me the undivided love of your's. It has long pained me to doubt the sincerity of your declarations, but I feel it due to myself to remonstrate with you. You are aware that is only my anxiety to hasten the day of our union that keeps me away from your side so much, as my uncle will not take me into

So let's dive in.

HOW TO
BE A PEN PAL

FAMOUS

*Jean-Paul Sartre and
Simone de Beauvoir*

*Edith Wharton and
Henry James*

*Elizabeth Bishop and
Robert Lowell*

*Groucho Marx
and T. S. Eliot*

During the brief, giddy time of the pandemic, between the vaccines and a new variant wave circa fall 2021, I made the truly batty decision to host Thanksgiving dinner for twenty. I hadn't socialized with that many people at once in nearly two years, but I suddenly felt an urge to orchestrate an old-fashioned, messy feast with wine sloshing everywhere, candle wax melting onto the tablecloths, and greasy fingertips reaching for seconds—plus a punch bowl and friends running out to the bodega to grab four more sticks of butter and strangers meeting across a platter of biscuits. My parents flew across the country to be there, as did my partner's family. Friends streamed in all day from all corners of the city. It was a *lot*. I may or may not have broken into tears when a broiler-meets-yams accident set off the fire alarm. But even inside the vortex of putting together a meal for two dozen and realizing every step of the way that I had bitten off far more hostessing than I could chew, one thought kept me humming along as the day approached: *I was going to meet my pen pal. I was going to meet Amy.*

Amy is a certified nurse-midwife who lives in Chicago in a sunny condo with her rascally rescue cattle dog, Bolo. She has long dusty-blonde hair that she usually wears in a braid tossed over one shoulder, or tucked into a scrub cap when she is delivering a baby. She works at a community hospital with mostly low-income patients and she is phenomenally devoted to her mission of advocating for pregnant people's wants and needs, despite a crushing health-care system that rarely supports new parents, particularly those from underserved communities. She regularly slips out of bed at three in the morning

PEN PALS

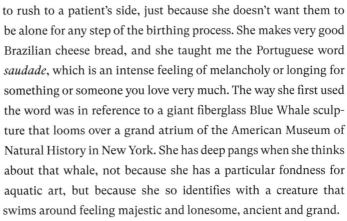

*Zora Neale Hurston and
Langston Hughes*

*Alfred Stieglitz and
Georgia O'Keeffe*

*Truman Capote and
Patricia Highsmith*

*Ralph Ellison and
Shirley Jackson*

to rush to a patient's side, just because she doesn't want them to be alone for any step of the birthing process. She makes very good Brazilian cheese bread, and she taught me the Portuguese word *saudade*, which is an intense feeling of melancholy or longing for something or someone you love very much. The way she first used the word was in reference to a giant fiberglass Blue Whale sculpture that looms over a grand atrium of the American Museum of Natural History in New York. She has deep pangs when she thinks about that whale, not because she has a particular fondness for aquatic art, but because she so identifies with a creature that swims around feeling majestic and lonesome, ancient and grand.

I learned all of these things about Amy from reading her letters.

Amy and I have been writing to each other, more or less weekly, for almost four years (and it will be much longer by the time this book emerges). We found each other in an unceremonious way—Amy sent me a message on Twitter, shortly before I launched the PenPalooza project and had casually posed the idea of writing letters to strangers to pass the time in early lockdown. "I'm up for it!" she wrote, and even though we didn't know each other, I sent her my address in hopes that she might be serious. She was.

What I got from her was unlike any letter I had ever received—long, conspiratorial, full of handwritten recipes and sense memories and poetic asides. It was like we had already been writing for decades. She inspired me to raise my letter game in order to keep up with her beautiful words, and I found myself staying up into the wee hours on summer nights typing out long notes on my typewriter. After starting with letters, we began sending books and trinkets and pictures of trees from strolls around our respective cities. One day, Amy shipped me a huge, heavy ceramic planter that she had made, and I put my favorite philodendron in it. I sent Amy a crumb cake and a dozen Brazilian Brigadeiro cookies. She sent me an enormous monstera plant.

For the first year of our friendship, we only communicated via mailbox. We didn't call. We didn't text. We barely messaged each other on social media, only sending a brief note here and there to assure the other that a letter was in the mail. Then, one summer, when I was changing apartments and so frazzled by the process that I needed to talk to someone who knew me almost better than anyone else, I finally punched Amy's number into my phone. Her voice—gravelly, warm, soothing—was just like her writing. Soon we were texting every day and calling each other to pass the time on long walks. And then, on a whim, she booked a ticket to New York for Thanksgiving.

I don't know quite how to explain it, but when Amy and I met face-to-face for the first time on the street outside my apartment, we embraced like long-lost sisters. We walked together around Brooklyn for hours that day, talking about everything and nothing. We sat on park benches, we got multiple coffees. We'd already said so much in our letters, and yet there were no awkward silences.

Our letter-writing project has been all about a kind of radical acceptance—perhaps we felt like we could tell each other anything *because* we began as total strangers. On Thanksgiving, Amy was the party MVP: She lugged cases of wine, she circulated around the room and talked to anyone who looked lost, she led the kitchen cleanup crew, she stayed until after midnight in order to flop down on the couch and recap the evening. None of this surprised me. She is exactly the generous, kind, curious person that she is in her letters. As it turns out, long-term epistolary relationships are perhaps the best way to get to know someone to their core.

I lucked out with Amy—as I did with a few other regular pen pals I write to—but I had no idea at first what our letter-writing would bring. That first envelope in the mail was a leap of faith, like a bizarre form of blind dating. It could have absolutely gone another way; we could have sent a few stale letters and slowly let our communication trickle to a stop. Several of my attempts at pen palling over the years have fizzled and failed or simply gone cold out of nowhere. Just before I turned thirteen, I met a girl at summer camp named

Elizabeth who called herself Letty and who ruled over our bunk with confident charisma. At the end of the summer, she promised to write me letters for a whole year. I felt like I had hit the correspondence jackpot. For a few months, we traded envelopes we made out of ripped pages from the dELiA*s catalog or *Seventeen* (hey, it was the '90s). But as the pressures of junior high rushed in, letters became less and less frequent, and then one day they merely stopped coming.

I was devastated by the suddenly empty mailbox—perhaps it is what made me continue to seek them out throughout my life. In college, I studied abroad and sent long letters back home. When I moved to New York, I sent letters to friends who had stayed on the West coast. But it wasn't until the pandemic hit—and really until Amy sent me that message—that I finally found someone who was as excited as I was about beginning a Very Long Correspondence. Maybe it was the sudden lack of human interaction, maybe it was sheer boredom of being indoors, but the first few months of our correspondence had the frenzied energy and passion you'd find in a Regency romance.

Pen palling—writing back and forth with someone as a conscious, consistent practice—can get a bad rap, at least among adults. It is often seen as a juvenile activity, a holdover from the days when your World Studies teacher made you write an awkward letter to another student across the globe. The term *pen pal* itself, which came into common parlance in the 1930s, sounds unserious and, I'm sorry to say, uncool (I far prefer the term *pen-friend*, which was in heavy rotation around the 1910s but soon fell out of fashion). I never quite know what to call Amy when I talk about her. If I say, "Oh, she's my pen pal!" I'll often get a strange look, as if someone cannot believe that a woman in her late thirties still has *pen pals*. But as there is no better word to describe this strange relationship, I have learned to embrace it. For centuries, humans of all ages have written letters to one another—letters about love and death and intrigue and invention and sex and war and heartbreak and illness and forgiveness. If anything, I think more adults could benefit from finding an Amy. It has improved my life immensely to have someone whose words I can read late at night, when I can sit in a big chair and get to know more about her

and then make myself a cup of tea (or mix a Negroni) and take out a fresh sheet of paper to answer while her thoughts are still fresh in my mind. It is both a slow and urgent form of friendship.

Whenever I feel a bit silly about how much my epistolary relationships mean to me, I think about the great chef Julia Child, who had the same pen pal for most of her adult life. When Julia first wrote to Avis DeVoto in 1951, she didn't even know that she was doing so. To explain: Julia, who had moved to Paris in 1948 with her husband Paul, who worked for the State Department (the two met when they were both working for the Office of Strategic Services in Sri Lanka during World War II), had fallen into a second act as an obsessive cook. After taking a basic course at Le Cordon Bleu, Julia was soon cooking circles around the male gourmands, and she joined the Circle des Gourmettes, which historian Joan Reardon, who collected Child's and Devoto's letters in her 2010 book *As Always, Julia*, described as an "exclusive club started in the late 1920s" dedicated to women and gastronomy. It was through this club that she began collaborating with two other women on a manuscript that would serve as an introduction to French cuisine for American home cooks.

But even before she started writing the book that would become *Mastering the Art of French Cooking*, Julia began forming a lot of staunch culinary opinions. She had ideas about how to chop mushrooms, when to buy fish, and about which knives were overrated. When she read an article in *Harper's* called "Crusade Resumed" by the Boston-based journalist Bernard DeVoto about how stainless steel knives were poorly made and could not stay sharp for long enough, she found herself nodding in emphatic agreement. And so, in March of 1952, she wrote DeVoto a letter telling him that she applauded his hot take. A month later, Bernard's wife, Avis, a book editor, wrote back instead. "I hope you won't mind hearing from me instead of my husband," she wrote, but assured Julia that she spoke for them both. "On the subject of cutlery," she wrote, "we are in entire agreement." She went on to thank Julia for a knife she had sent from France, which her husband used for "cutting the lemon peel for the proper thickness for the six-o-clock Martini." And a lasting pen pal–ship was born.

> "This afternoon we start for the wild west to be gone about a week and I hope to find a letter from you on our return."
>
> —Willa Cather to George Seibel and Helen Hiller Seibel, 1897

Julia and Avis wrote 120 letters to each other before they met. In her second letter to Avis, Julia sent her own recipe for "Veau à la Crème, à l'Estragon," veal in a heavy cream sauce with shallots and tarragon. "Recipes noted," Avis wrote back, and then began to sprinkle in delightful musings about food and memory. She writes of the egg dish called "Pipérade" that "I really cannot think of any dish more suited to a quivering stomach after too much wine the night before! Not that I ate it as a hangover cure; I have not had a hangover in fifteen years, thank you." Julia soon began sending Avis manuscript pages from her book in progress, telling her to keep them top secret. Still, Avis did not exactly keep this material to herself—she shared it with the publisher Houghton Mifflin. The publishing house rejected the initial manuscript—big mistake, huge!—so Avis helped to move the book to Knopf, where it was turned into a national bestseller.

Over the years, Avis and Julia shared professional dreams and fears, meandering thoughts on marriage, whispered secrets, family gossip, bitchy asides about bad American cooking technique, gripes about the backward publishing business, and countless recipes involving plenty of butter and good olive oil. When the two finally met for the first time in Boston in 1954, much like myself and Amy, they greeted each other like lifelong friends—one very tall and one petite. And that is what they remained. "I feel that I can communicate more readily and freely with you than anyone in the world," Avis wrote to Julia. Julia responded in kind, writing about how nice it was to get to know someone purely through their letters and to form a "passionate" friendship via the mail. In each other they not only found a like mind, but someone who was game for a good long volley.

Julia Child was a late bloomer in nearly every way. She didn't marry until she was thirty-four (which was considered practically an old maid in 1946). She didn't find her life's calling until she was in her late thirties. She didn't publish her first book until she was in her forties. She didn't star in her own TV show until she was fifty-one. What I have learned from her, and from her gregarious correspondence with Avis over the years, is that it is never too late to change course or try something new. This includes being a pen pal! It is not just for teenagers or fan club presidents. It might just be for you.

HOW TO WRITE YOUR
VERY FIRST LETTER

To begin with, take a deep breath. Accept the fact that, despite your serious intentions, you are essentially doing something a little bit silly, a little bit anachronistic, and a little bit melodramatic. Accept the fact that your first letter is going to feel awkward and stilted and not like your best work. Accept the fact that in the modern age, very few people write by hand any longer, let alone for another person to read, and that your scribbles may be semi-indecipherable. But also know that your letter, no matter its legibility or coherence, will be met with absolute excitement.

Whatever you put in the mail, even if it does not rise to the great epistolary heights that you someday hope to emulate, is still a surprise on its way to enliven someone's dreary mailbox.

So let go of the pressure. Just begin. If you're feeling overwhelmed, start with a short postcard or a simple note on creamy stationery in which you say hello, explain a bit about yourself and why you want to start writing more letters, and offer up a few evocative details from the past season (Did you travel? Welcome a pet or family member? Grow a particularly beautiful zucchini in your garden? Take up a hobby? Discover an amazing way to roast fennel?). You don't have to go into too much detail or divulge all of your

> "Letters are above all useful as a means of expressing the ideal self; and no other method of communication is quite so good for this purpose."

> —*Elizabeth Hardwick,*
> *in an essay about literary*
> *correspondence, 1953*

ancestral wisdom in the first round—it's best to leave something to the imagination and give your correspondences some breathing room to grow richer and more trusting over time.

In general, I think a short letter is a perfect way to begin; it won't intimidate your reader or make them feel that they must write a long letter in return. That said, if you are more of a maximalist when it comes to first impressions—if you are the type to burst into parties carrying Champagne and a boombox—I believe there is no downside to really *going for it* on your first effort. So many of my favorite first letters were very long (one person I still write to started out by sending me twenty-five pages!) and full of quirks and diversions and strange asides. I feel instantly closer to those who write a lot—and in turn they inspire me to write more in my own letters. Effort inspires effort.

Send out the kind of letter you would want to receive. Do you want a rapid flurry of lighthearted, easygoing short updates? Great! Do you want an emotional exchange of thoughts and feelings and deepest fears? Lead with vulnerability and openness! Do you want someone to send funky snacks and strange ephemera to—and vice versa? Get weird with it! The energy you put into your first letter will almost always come back to you like a boomerang. This is your chance to set the tone of the kind of correspondence you want to have. Don't stress—you can always evolve later. But why not come out swinging?

HOW TO WRITE
A FAN LETTER

"Fan mail" is—let's face it—a little bit embarrassing. The words *fan letter* bring to mind twelve-year-olds scribbling gushy love notes to pop stars in spiral notebooks while snapping watermelon bubblegum. And while I have a great tenderness for the gum snappers—I was one myself, having written dozens of as-yet-unanswered valentines to actors and singers in my Lisa Frank binder era—writing letters of admiration does not have to end after adolescence. I'm not talking about traditional "omigodiluvyou-somuch" letters that fan clubs collect and send in big batches to whatever army of assistants is responsible for sorting a celebrity's mail, but more substantive and reflective notes of praise to those who have created something or done something that made your world feel a bit bigger or your loneliness feel a bit smaller.

I might argue that this is one of the most timeless and enduring uses for sending mail, one that doesn't feel outmoded or kitschy, but still vital and useful. Because (and this is a little secret I will let you in on), most artists/writers/actors/dancers/designers/etc., unless they are quite famous, don't really hear all that often from those they are trying to reach. Obviously, pop stars who can fill stadiums and best-selling authors who have sold millions of copies still get old-timey burlap sacks groaning with mail and fan art and glitter. Your letter might not make a dent there, and it's not ever guaranteed that anyone will even open it. (Though who knows? David Bowie regularly answered fan mail out of the blue throughout his career.) What I am talking about is writing to people working at a more terrestrial level: first-time novelists, character actors, poets, indie filmmakers, painters, theater performers, photographers, journalists, illustrators, activists, podcast hosts. In my experience, most people working in this

capacity—that is, struggling to make a creative life—regularly wonder if what they are doing is connecting, and regularly think about quitting altogether to do something else. A little note, even if it is just to say, "What you wrote or said or made mattered to me," can be endlessly encouraging, even if you never hear back. I am a staunch believer in writing such notes right away, in the moment when you feel most acutely grateful for and excited about whatever work someone is making. The second I close a book or read a piece that I truly loved, I start working on a little letter to the author saying so. I know that such notes have buoyed me when I needed it most.

If you need some extra encouragement, know that writing fan mail puts you in dazzling company: George Clooney apparently writes letters every day, often to his idols (which is how he ended up pen-palling with Walter Cronkite and Paul Newman). Prince wrote letters to Joni Mitchell when he was a teenager and sent them via her fan club. (Her staff, apparently, thought his long odes were the work of someone on the "lunatic fringe" and threw them away; years later Mitchell would call him "the best performer I have ever witnessed.") In the 1960s, Nina Simone and Langston Hughes maintained a correspondence that read like a series of mutual fan letters. In one letter, Simone gushed to Hughes that she planned to go out and buy every book he had ever written.

There are some ground rules for fan mail outside of a swoony teenage context—let's call this "admiration mail"—and they are unwavering: Don't be a creep. Don't talk about someone's appearance. Keep the focus on the work and keep the letter brief. Write a few sentences about what you found meaningful, say thank you, and leave it at that. Cite a line, a lyric, a brushstroke, a monologue, or even an emailed newsletter that made you feel something. The more specific you can be, the more the note will read like a direct and deliberate engagement with the work. Don't send the letter to someone's home, even if you can google their personal address (unless they are a friend of a friend or someone you could plausibly meet around town, then you can ask your mutual acquaintance permission to send a note along).

This is not the fan mail of yore, where the goal was getting a signed headshot or a radio shout-out. There should be no goal, or even a hope for a reply. This is more of an open-ended ode, putting gratitude and enthusiasm into the universe as its own end; a generous act that requires no reciprocation. This can be tough, because you will often never know if your note landed, or had an effect, or even if it was ever read. But that's not the point. I try to reply to every kind note I've received from strangers about something I've written, but sometimes I am too in the weeds of my own process to do so. Still, the notes have kept me going when I wanted to stop, and have been a beacon when I couldn't see a way forward. You have to trust that just by caring enough to write the note in the first place, you are doing something meaningful, even if you never hear back (but then again, as Bowie proved, you just might).

This is, it should be said, all about writing to total strangers—there are, of course, fan letters you can write to people already in your orbit that will have a more direct

SINCERELY CONSIDER . . .

WRITING TO STRANGERS

If you have the letter-writing bug and have exhausted yourself on sending out fan letters, consider looking into a correspondence program that will pair you with a stranger who could really use some mail. There are many nonprofit and volunteer programs that can match you with the elderly, the sick, the incarcerated, the lonely, or anyone else who could use a little pick-me-up. Some of the resources listed below have a political or activist bent to them, and some do not. I encourage you to look into these and other programs to find the right fit for you—mail can be someone's conduit to the outside world or the only human communication they have from someone for weeks.

- The Last Prisoner Project
- The Letter Project
- Girls Love Mail
- Any Refugee
- Letters against Depression
- Letters against Isolation
- Love for Our Elders
- Letters to Strangers
- The World Needs More Love Letters
- Cards for Hospitalized Kids
- Prisoner Correspondence Project
- Operation Gratitude
- Black and Pink LGBTQ Letters Project

and, likely, reciprocal response. And you should be writing those, too. Write to a schoolteacher who changed the course of your life. Write to a friend who just published her first big essay. Write to one of your online mutuals who makes your life better, and not worse, when you log on in the morning. Write to an old college roommate whose baby pictures you double-tap on Instagram but whose greater impact on your life you've never really expressed. Write to the best coworker you ever had and thank her for getting you through pointless meetings with her sense of humor. Write to a person who was kind to you when they did not have to be, even if it was years ago. If you are still thinking about it, it belongs in a letter. Write freely and generously, on thick stationery (or in someone's DMs, though that's a far less dignified way to go). It may feel strange at first, but soon it will start to feel like a regular practice. Believe me, there are worse things in life than to be known as the person who is always sending out lovely notes.

In an essay called "The Case for Writing Fan Mail" in the *New York Times*, a doctor named Rachael Bedard explained why she keeps writing fan letters, for the thrill of communing in a new way with someone or something that made life feel a bit sparklier and worth slogging through. "The thrill was in my writing, in putting my adoration into words," she writes. "The romance of the confession depends on holding nothing back."

Finnish artist Tove Jansson once wrote a short story, called "Messages," using fragments of fan letters and missives she penned to her partner, Tooti.

"Hi coming later heat the soup" [. . .]
"My hamsters have been named after you and your brother" [. . .] "I'm Margit, the one who punched you in the stomach in the playground."

HOW TO WRITE
ABOUT THE WEATHER

If you live in a place where the seasons change, even a little bit, then you are likely familiar with a phenomenon that pops up out of nowhere a few times a year and which marks the passing of time like an invisible metronome. Clicking, clicking. This undeniable marker of time is, of course, the inevitable Day of the Wrong Coat. I don't know of any better weather vane, or a more consistent way to tell that one season is slowly melting into another, than stepping out into the street and realizing, with a shock, that you have chosen completely inappropriate outerwear for the occasion.

In New York City, for example, this day tends to fall sometime around early March. You set out on a long stroll in your heavy winter woolens, ready to turn your collar up against brittle winds, and instead find that it is gray but secretly balmy out, the air heavy and thick and almost curdled. All the wool does is enhance the general wet-dog sensation, and you are left wandering around with sweat dripping down your back. The Day of the Wrong Coat happens yet again in mid-May, when you try to push a leather bomber jacket as far as it can go before you must peel it off your sticky elbows and schlep it around, the garment bulging out of a tote bag or slung awkwardly over one arm like a maître d's towelette. And it happens yet again sometime in September, when you leave the apartment in a light tweed blazer, thinking you are living out a breezy, rust-tinted, *When Harry Met Sally* Meg Ryan–esque, Central Park leaf-peeping fantasy, but mostly you are shivering and cursing your decision not to bring a scarf.

The Day of the Wrong Coat always involves some level of discomfort, but it is not wholly unpleasant. It is more than anything a day about noticing, about realizing that the winds are shifting and the crocuses are

NTRA

THE DRIVE.

getting ready to bloom. I always look forward to these moments of flux, even if it means dragging a ten-pound faux fur teddy bear coat with me between boroughs like it is a giant stuffed animal I won at an arcade. The point is to feel the tension, to clock the discord between the weather and your imaginative idea of what the weather should be. There is a bracing, humbling humanness to not planning well; there is clarity in the cacophonous, mismatched rhythms of expectation and reality.

Think about the last time you wore an outfit that made you feel out of step with the elements. What was your most recent Day of the Wrong Coat? It might make a good subject for a letter.

Writing about the weather in correspondence has somehow become seen as a lazy method of throat-clearing or a cheat to stretch out a letter's length. I know this because people tend to apologize over and over in their letters for doing it—many of the notes I receive include glorious descriptions of sunsets and rainstorms followed by a "Sorry I just spent a paragraph writing about what I can see outside my window!" But I say: Go for it.

Where else to write about what you see outside your window than to someone in another place, with another window onto a view they can then write you back about? There are depths to plumb from simply shooting the breeze about the breeze in your letters; from wandering through the woods and noting how the morning light looked diffused through the canopy, from lying on a patch of summer grass and recording its milky, vegetal scent. Writing about the ways that the weather affects you—the way the sun feels on your bare limbs, the way that cold feels in your lungs, the way that the rain releases petrichor from the pavement and in doing so also releases an unplanned blue funk—can feel like literary stalling, but it doesn't have to be that way. In fact, writing about the weather and all of its attendant sensual pleasures—how a summer afternoon smells (chlorine, melted cherry snow cones, honeyed lilac blossoms, sea salt, coconut pulp) or sounds (the ebb and flow of waves, the steady cadence of a garden sprinkler, the honking of taxicabs stuck in humid traffic, the bass beats of a pop song pulsating from a stranger's backyard)—is really a sly and elegant excuse to write about yourself.

THE COVE.

I love letters about the seasons. They allow writers to write about beauty and terror without saying, "Here I am, writing about beauty and terror." They lend themselves to metaphor: blooming flowers for fresh love; overcast skies for inertia and frustration; honeyed, languid humidity for yearning and unrequited crushes; snowfall for the fresh beginnings that can only come after a period of deep hibernation. We are all so affected by what happens in the air around us, especially in these times of extreme heat and sudden storms, so why not pour those feelings into a letter? If anything, you will be creating a useful archive of climate reporting for future generations.

A great place to begin, when writing a letter about the weather, is to complain about it. Perhaps, as in the case of Willa Cather, writing in 1905, the winter cold has made you feel lethargic and bored:

I have a week's vacation the last of March and I am hoping to go to New York then. One gets so terribly in the rut here in the winter, though, that one's rather timid about venturing out. I don't know whether you've ever been in a grind long enough to realize what that feeling is, and how stupid and flat and dull it makes people. You get to wanting to stay home just to hide your own dullness—you're so afraid you'll be found out and your shameful nakedness exposed. [My friend] Isabelle frequently threatens to drug me and put me in a Pullman and ship me off for parts unknown, so that I'll have to waken up and use my wits. So I may arrive in New York in a semi-conscious state sometime in the last week of March.

Or perhaps the summer swelter has made you feel lovelorn and melancholy, a feeling that the South African novelist Bessie Head wrote about so beautifully in a letter to a friend.

> For no particular reason a long, dry, thundery,
> brooding summer wrapped itself around me. It never
> rained. And the mood of the weather began to explain
> many other things for me. I think the mind picks
> on anything to explain the brooding of the heart;
> sometimes a love affair, sometimes a soul journey to
> the end of the universe but many other things get
> explained along the way.

Another method is to go the pure rhapsody route: to wax enchanted about the natural world with the enthusiasm and wonder of a pastoral poet who has a picnic basket full of juicy adjectives. Here again is Bessie Head, this time describing the euphoric flip side of summer's bounty, the "rush of growth" of ripe tomatoes:

> We are really having a glorious summer with rain on
> the horizon. And if it really rains what a lot of
> food, pumpkin, watermelon, cabbage, spinach, green
> onions, tomatoes. The early rain is a surprise
> because this time of the year is hell. Hot dry wind
> storms from the desert. Hot, baking days. First time
> summer came in so magnificently, since I've been
> here. First time gardeners get such good luck one
> can almost feel the rush of growth in the garden.

The outdoors are a gift when you don't know what to write about, because they allow you to lean into contrast and dissonance. Perhaps it is an absolutely gorgeous day outside and you feel like garbage. Perhaps the clouds are sending down a thrashing sleet and it makes no sense at all because you feel giddy. One day, you will feel completely in concert with the weather, as if the sky is a mirror reflecting back your mood. Other days, you will feel like an untuned, warped violin. Exploring

these feelings of congruousness and discord—that's the stuff of a good letter. Here's the British writer Vita Sackville-West describing a trip to the Italian Riviera that would be lovely and "delicious in warm weather," but looks "simply silly" in a blizzard.

> Presently we shall walk into Rapallo, our heads held down against the blizzard, to fetch such letters as may be at the hotel. It was such a beastly hotel. We found this tiny villa on Monday when we were out for a walk; it would be delicious in warm weather, for it is practically *in* the sea, and from the windows you can see right down the coast as far as Spezia. Did I tell you this? I forget. But now the sea lashes the rock on which it is built, and the oranges look simply silly. Southern countries look much sillier in wintry weather than northern ones do in summery. I don't quite know what I mean by that, but I know I mean something.

My favorite part is the end: "I don't quite know what I mean by that, but I know I mean something." I love when a letter includes a big swing, a half-developed idea. Why does Liguria, with its citrus trees and jutting cliffs and fisherman's cottages look "so much sillier in wintry weather" than England looks in high summer? Perhaps she's working toward a grand theory about the persistent power of fantasy; the Portofino Coast of Sackville-West's mind is a land of perennial neroli and fig trees, a place of rejuvenation and warmth. To be there in a blizzard is to know that the cold can follow you anywhere, that the cosmic joke of escape is that sometimes you end up with wet socks in a beastly hotel, fetching letters from the place you left behind.

Cultivating Seasonal Obsessions

A tip: Seasons don't necessarily have to correlate to the weather—you can create your own. One of the best ways to have something new to write about in your letters is to remain curious, but it is easy to let the mind atrophy and settle into the same old patterns and the same old dent in the sofa, as you're streaming the same old show about flipping houses.

So here is a trick that a mentor of mine once told me: Pick a new guiding obsession for every season. It could be a word, a color, an actor, a genre of music, a slice of film history, a sport, an ingredient, an animal, a poet, a smell, a flower, an artist, a historical period, a city . . . anything. It doesn't matter how ridiculous it is, or how obscure, or how small. I like to write whatever I pick on a sticky note and slap it over my desk. Then, start to curate a seasonal engagement with the idea, privately and purposefully, as if you were in charge of putting together a class syllabus or a cultural festival dedicated to this specific thing. Read books about it, watch films that mention it or evoke it, put together playlists that remind you of it, seek out perfumes that smell like it, wear outfits that put you in the mood for it.

Suddenly, you will start to refract the entire world through the lens of this one theme, and you will begin to make connections you never saw before. You'll find yourself seeking out books you wouldn't have read, places you wouldn't have visited, foods you wouldn't have tried. The key is, once the season is over, you take down the sticky note. You send someone a long letter about your favorite discoveries of the past few months, and then you put up a brand-new Post-it and start hunting all over again. Think of it as an intentional curiosity safari. The seasons keep changing, and so will you. And now, you have something to write about.

To Every Letter, There Is a Season

New York City summers can be glorious, but most days are sticky and gray and seem to last a thousand years. There are stretches—the languid, soupy weeks where late July turns into early August—when the air feels thick and viscous, and beverages sweat so heavily that you cannot set them near electronics. Houseplants bake to a crisp in windowsills and the only foods that taste right are frozen blueberries and half-sour pickles straight from the tub. It rains and you think it's going to provide some relief, but instead it just turns your whole body into one of those rental lake houses where everything is limp and mildewed. These are the weeks when the only thing to do on a Sunday afternoon is plop yourself near the A/C unit and dive into some activity that doesn't require you to move; to me it is a perfect time to write letters while you work your way through a bowl of ice-cold cherries.

The writer, proto-influencer, and consummate New York "It girl" Zelda Fitzgerald, who only lived in Manhattan a little while but who seemed to chase summertime around the world throughout her life, wrote far better than I ever could about this period in her own correspondence. She was always at her best when scribbling her way through slow, over-heated afternoons. In July 1939, she wrote: "Summer billows over the sky and the lakes; every green square swoons to the sway of a white swirling dress . . ." In August of 1938, she wrote of a "vaporous heat of a wet summer" that "threatened to hatch all sorts of things." In 1937, writing to her husband Scott from a hospital in Ashland, she speaks of a place where "apple orchards slumber down the hill-sides."

All writers seem to have seasons in which they bloom, like isolated perennials. Edith Wharton wrote best about the winter, because she wrote about rich people, the only people who think January is the best

time because their indoor space is so expansive that it might as well be outdoors, and because they have roaring fireplaces, and because they have furs and hot whiskey drinks and bespangled muffs or whatever other Gilded Age folderol she wrote about. James Baldwin seemed to write in perpetual Parisian springtime, with the bracing air of a morning balcony. Walt Whitman was an autumn poet; so was Sylvia Plath, whose "Black Rook in Rainy Weather" is basically a poem about how fall makes you walk around in the sort of moony haze where you think birds are miracles when maybe they might just be birds.

In any case, Zelda's words belong to summer, no matter what month it was when she wrote them. They are often overripe and straining at the edges, like a magnolia in full June bloom. Which is to say: She wrote dramatically and fragrantly about the weather, as if the state of the sky were the great drama of her life.

Zelda was not always in a peaceful place when she wrote these letters. She sent out many of her best notes while living at mental health facilities in Switzerland and North Carolina. Her letters—many of which are collected in the book *Dear Scott, Dearest Zelda*, edited by Jackson R. Bryer and Cathy W. Barks (a must-have for any letters enthusiast)—tend to look backward to a time when she was roaming around Paris or crashing parties or living out of hotels with Scott in the 1920s. There is a melancholy, elegiac quality to them, as she splashes around in old memories. But the letters are also vitally alive and attuned to the present moment, and you see that in

her weather reports. She manages to experience every rain shower as an ecstatic event.

Zelda's epistolary writing about the seasons remains some of the most exuberant and irrepressible work I have read; I encourage you to seek it out if you want to be reminded that writing about the weather does not have to be boring. It can be intoxicating. It can be operatic. It can be humid and blustery and as refreshing as cold stone fruit. So look outside. Pull out some paper and some sumptuous adjectives and write someone a letter about what you see.

BONJOUR !
CHAPEAU, DE CAMILLE ROGER

Nº 4 de la Gazette du Bon Ton.   Année 1921. — Planche 27

THE BACK PORCH

488 3rd Ave.

a pencil for your thoughts

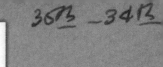
3513 _ 3413

NEW YORK. FROM HOBOKEN

EIMS

The Waldorf-Astoria
A Hilton Hotel

BE SAFE CLOSE COVER BEFORE STRIKING

N. Y. TIME
PROMOTION AD   SERVIC
7th FLOOR
WOZN

TONIGHT

Plaza Hotel, New York.

A SMALL SEASONAL VOCABULARY

Most conventional writing advice tells you to never reach for a $10 word when a dollar word will do . . . but letters just so happen to be a place where you get to throw out conventional writing advice. It's your letter! Pack it with $50 words if you want! Writing about the weather is a great excuse to use some luxurious adjectives. Here are some of my favorite words for all seasons.

WINTER

- Glacial
- Siberian
- Hibernal
- Polar
- Cocoon
- Hearthside
- Nippy
- Slush
- Rime
- Hoarfrost
- Velvety
- Swaddled
- Torpid
- Gelid
- Apricity

SPRING

- Vernal
- Plumule
- Sprout
- Bloom
- Jonquil
- Deluge
- Petrichor
- Redolent
- Millpond
- Efflorescence
- Renaissance
- Flush
- Burgeoning
- Fecund
- Effulgence

PASADENA, CAL.

SUMMER

- Torrid
- Balmy
- Fevered
- Sultry
- Clammy
- Languid
- Slothful
- Sizzle
- Fragrant
- Muggy
- Lush
- Chartreuse
- Honeyed
- Verdant
- Fractious

AUTUMN

- Crisp
- Umber
- Harvest
- Aureate
- Rust
- Marmalade
- Ginger
- Tawny
- Ochre
- Crumbly
- Brisk
- Sepia
- Bracing
- Brambly
- Russet

Maybe your seasonal obsession is with
learning how to bake . . . or with
making the perfect gimlet . . . in which
case, you will need to know . . .

HOW TO
MAIL A RECIPE

The first time someone sent me a handwritten recipe through the mail—one of my longtime correspondents wrote her time-tested method for chewy chocolate-cherry cookies in loopy cursive on a lined index card and slipped it gingerly between the folds of a longer letter—it felt like a revelation. It seemed so familial, as if she had passed on a delicate heirloom for my safekeeping.

Of course, recipes are not very hard to come by these days. If you search for WHITE BEAN STEW on the Internet, thousands of results pop up from thousands of food bloggers, often accompanied by personal stories about a grandmother's signature soup or a lean summer spent squatting in a studio apartment and surviving on canned cannellinis. Open a few more tabs and you can find a panoply of vetted recipes from industry professionals that are scientifically *proven* to work. The pros know the exact moment a bean morphs from firm to toothsome in hot liquid and can tell you with utmost confidence when to add a handful of shredded Parmesan to the broth so that it adds a silky, subtle kick of umami but does not become a gelatinous blob. And then there is the wide world of cookbooks, which are plentiful and beautiful to behold. It might be tempting to think that if you include a recipe in a letter it will get lost, because, well, who needs another foolproof carbonara hack when you have a dozen already at your fingertips?

Still, there is something *different* about a private recipe, one that is only meant for one person to read and to follow. There is an undeniable joy in cooking from someone else's words, especially knowing that you can report back the results to an eager audience. Food is so ephemeral and so personal—nobody else can really taste what you are tasting—and yet there has long been an undeniable impulse to *share* our meals, both literally and literarily. It makes sense that recipe-sharing would seep into

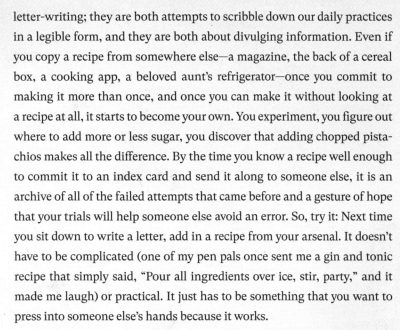

letter-writing; they are both attempts to scribble down our daily practices in a legible form, and they are both about divulging information. Even if you copy a recipe from somewhere else—a magazine, the back of a cereal box, a cooking app, a beloved aunt's refrigerator—once you commit to making it more than once, and once you can make it without looking at a recipe at all, it starts to become your own. You experiment, you figure out where to add more or less sugar, you discover that adding chopped pistachios makes all the difference. By the time you know a recipe well enough to commit it to an index card and send it along to someone else, it is an archive of all of the failed attempts that came before and a gesture of hope that your trials will help someone else avoid an error. So, try it: Next time you sit down to write a letter, add in a recipe from your arsenal. It doesn't have to be complicated (one of my pen pals once sent me a gin and tonic recipe that simply said, "Pour all ingredients over ice, stir, party," and it made me laugh) or practical. It just has to be something that you want to press into someone else's hands because it works.

One persistent piece of New York writerly lore is that the filmmaker and enthusiastic foodie Nora Ephron wrote a secret cookbook that she only shared with friends and neighbors. It was—according to whispers from those who claim to have seen a copy—full of quippy, gossipy commentary about salad dressing and baked chicken. I believe it exists, mostly because I think that Ephron, despite being a very public person, understood the power of clandestine communication. She did write the film *You've Got Mail*, after all. There is something irresistible about knowing that you can relay your kitchen triumphs and failures in a space free from judgment or expectation. The late food writer Laurie Colwin, whose *Gourmet* magazine columns in the 1980s and 1990s always felt like letters from a wisecracking older sister who was winningly bossy with a wooden spoon, wrote in her book *Home Cooking* that even disastrous meals can teach us something. "There is something triumphant about a really disgusting meal," she wrote in the novel. Letters are the perfect place to share your most disgusting triumphs. The cakes that collapsed, the mashed potatoes that tasted like Mod Podge. It will bring you closer to whoever you are writing to, and it will make them feel less alone.

RECIPE SUGGESTIONS

Maybe you don't cook! Put in a cocktail recipe! Don't drink? Put in a list of your must-have movie snacks! Handwritten recipes are surprisingly fun to receive in the mail. Here are some ideas for recipes and food-based lists to tuck into your next envelope:

What's Cookin?

ROMANCE!
FOOD! INTRIGUE!

Share your most seductive recipe. What meal could make someone fall in love with you?

I WANT CANDY!

Your best recipe involving pre-existing candy (I, for example, am not above infusing vodka with pink Starbursts and then using it to make a cosmopolitan; it is surprisingly delicious).

A FAMILY SECRET

This is the place to spill your grandmother's well-guarded brisket hack or the surprise ingredient in your aunt's curry. Go on, do it. We're all family here.

Time for a note!

DINNER PARTY MVP DISH

Your go-to, never fail, crowd-pleaser for when you have guests over. What is *your* version of the infamous Silver Palate Chicken Marbella?

COMFORT FOOD:

A recipe that feels like a bear hug. The dish that tastes like care to you, and the one you cook for the people you most care about.

A HOT BEV

Your signature steaming drink (alcoholic or non). Give it a name.

Here's what's cookin' *Your Twist on a Classic* Serves ___

Recipe from the kitchen of _____

Lasagna, à la you. Or share your own spin on eggs Benedict.

Your Madeleine Moment

A recipe that, when you make it, rockets you immediately into a sense memory. Write out the story behind the recipe in your next letter.

ALWAYS WORKS

A recipe that has never failed you. An old friend, a loyal friend.

NEVER WORKS

A recipe that always fails you, even when you need it most. And yet, you keep trying. One day, that soufflé will rise.

Contents

ONE FOR THE ARCHIVES

If you had to choose one recipe to pass down to future generations, which would it be? Send along a recipe that defines who you are when you step into the kitchen, for now and forever.

DIFFICULT BUT WORTH IT

The most labor-intensive recipe in your regular arsenal. We're talking sixty-ingredient cassoulet, croissants from scratch, a four-layer mousse cake, an all-day Bolognese that simmers slowly for hours. High risk, high reward.

TUESDAY GROCERIES DINNER

Imagine that you can only cook with what you can carry home from a quick trip to the market. Think: fresh produce, a baguette, some herbs, maybe a splurge-y cheese.

EASY SWEETNESS

Your lowest-hassle dessert. Think galettes, crumbles, icebox cakes.

Sunday Snack Attack

It's 9 p.m. on a Sunday and you are not ready for the weekend to be over. What can you toss together in the kitchen to extend your feeling of freedom for just a few more hours? Do you have a special sundae to ward off the scaries?

HOW TO WRITE
A LETTER LIKE A POET

Poets are simply better at writing letters than the rest of us. This makes sense—they have an epic advantage when it comes to noticing life's small but mighty details and then finding the perfect words to wrap around them. I think of the way that Elizabeth Bishop, in a letter to her friend and mentor Marianne Moore, described a group of pelicans she saw on a trip to Florida: "Most of them have brown heads, but once in a while you see one with what looks like a fine wig of peroxide blond." Or the way that Leslie Marmon Silko described an old hen she kept on her property in New Mexico in one of many letters she wrote to a man named James Wright (who first wrote to her on a whim after reading one of her books): "Her feathers are grimy oily gray." (Poets have a particular knack for describing birds.)

The letters of poets do not always contain discreet poetry (though in Sylvia Plath's case, she would often scribble stanzas on postcards and send them to her mother). What makes the letters interesting—and why I will always snatch up a collection of a poet's letters when I see one in a used bookstore—is seeing what happens when a poet, usually so tethered to working within the confines and structures of a specific form, gives themselves over to a place of epistolary freedom. In letters, poets can write in verse, or prose, or fragments. They can work in lists and limericks, long paragraphs and short sentences. You can feel a sense of adventure in many poets' letters, a kind of verbal mischief-making and an effort to push the rules. They want their letters to surprise and delight the receiver with the words they choose, even when they are receiving or delivering bad news. Take this excerpt from a letter from 1965, from the poet Anne Sexton to her friend, the writer Tillie Olsen. Sexton laments

the fact that Tillie has been under the weather, but never dips into baleful seriousness. Her cheeky use of parentheses gets me every time:

Dearly Tillie,

Your valentines received!

Read! Loved.

WHY DON'T TYPEWRITERS MAKE LITTLE HEARTS????

AND YOUR NEW YEAR'S CARD FOR MY NEW HOME,MY NEW PLACE

They (both cards, notes, actual things) mean a great deal.
Something to treasure. Your note says you are not feeling well!!
(But *your* book is. Hooray for the book) (that *is* important too).
How sorry I am to learn that you are not. Annie mentioned it too.
All my catholic friends offer up their sickness to God. I wish that I
Could offer it up to the Muse. Or to Rilke. R. has some good (fine)
Things to say on the subject. (as for me, I've got nothing to say but
LOVE) which is all right but not practical. When I hear you feel
Not well I say (simply) Oh shit!

But that's not very poetic.

Sexton pokes fun at her lack of poetic expression while at the same time expressing herself utterly as a poet (I would argue that "Why don't typewriters make little hearts???" is its own short poem); she has a sense of humor about both what is expected of her and about undercutting those expectations.

To write a letter like a poet, you need to channel the part of you that believes, deep down, that the point of writing to another person (as opposed to just calling or texting them) is to invite them to play with you, to serve up a linguistic volley that they will feel compelled to answer with

just as much energy as you pour into it. All poets—at least those who are working in the modern world, and not in the time of Ovid when poets were celebrities—know that their audience is limited and often niche, but that doesn't stop them from yearning to connect, from striving to mystify and magnify daily life. You must approach your letter-writing with the same generous (and fanatical) belief that the words you write, no matter how limited the audience, are an offering. Your words can offer beauty, comfort, shared sorrow, cathartic rage, hard-earned insight, refreshing strangeness, absurd silliness, peace—and often all of these things, all mixed up, at the same time. What is important is that you keep experimenting, keep playing. What would happen if you totally freed yourself from your idea of what a letter should look like? What part of the paper would you write on? What new forms could your thoughts take? What birds will you notice, and how will you let your imagination take flight?

Poets are, above all things, collectors—of words, of images, of fragmentary life experiences that they later remix and reassemble in new ways. Poetry, like letter-writing, is often considered to be an obscure literary art, the kind of thing that people chip away at despite its waxing irrelevance. But if you are a poetry reader, then you know just how alive the medium is, how dizzying it feels when you are inside a poem that grips you. So write letters with all the bluster of a poet who still believes that words are where the meat of living resides. The next time you have a letter to write, try walking around a few days before you do so, and thinking of yourself as a poet (though I promise you don't have to make your letters rhyme). Home in on noises, textures, tastes. Write down half-sentences in a notebook about conversations you overhear or a stressful workday's little indignities or the best and worst smells you encounter as you move through an afternoon. Gather information and stay attuned to the world. The letter that tumbles out at the end will feel rich and musical and lived in.

SINCERELY CONSIDER . . .

Embellishments

Letters may have stiff competition from email and DMs and group chats in terms of conveying information, but they remain unmatched when it comes to their potential to deliver a tangible, immersive experience. So, I say, lean all the way into it. Embellish the hell out of your correspondence—fill your envelopes with found objects and strange ephemera and opulent little delights for the senses. You can mail almost anything that lies flat—the only limitation is your creativity.

Some ideas for flat(ish) pizzazz to include in your correspondence follow. It is important to note here that I am not speaking about sending care packages (though there is a note on that on page 172) or filling up a bubble mailer with so much bulk that it won't fit into a standard mailbox slot. This is about smuggling small extras into a traditional envelope using only your ingenuity and perhaps an extra Forever stamp to account for weight. I like to keep all of my flats in a shoebox near my desk; you can buy tea bags and stickers in bulk, so you'll always have something to toss in at the last minute.

MAILING AN EXTRA-LARGE LETTER? Buy a sheet of "non-machinable" stamps at the post office and stick one or two on any envelope that has a few extra bumps or ridges in it; those stamps are specifically designed to go on mail that might not squeeze into the flat mail-sorting machine. When in doubt, pile on more postage.

♥ HOT TIP:

You can buy adhesive paper pockets online, the kind that libraries stick in the back of books to hold lending cards, and stick them to the inside of notecards—this turns a blah card into a folio that contains tchotchkes galore.

Some Flats to Collect and Consider

I have successfully mailed all these items using stamps and a mailbox, but you really never know what works until you try it! Why not give it a whirl? Worst case: Your letter comes right back to you.

PREWRAPPED TEA BAGS: Marvelously slim, keep forever, and come in thousands of varieties. I like to collect tea bags when traveling and mail them out one by one.

STICKERS: A kitschy throwback to childhood. People love a big, vinyl sticker, the kind you can throw on a laptop or a water bottle. If you want to send stickers from a sticker book, you can buy cheap glossy backing paper online that allows you to peel off and reuse what you stick onto it.

FOUND EPHEMERA: Ticket stubs, ornate wine labels, vintage photographs, recipe cards, fortune cookie inserts, promotional postcards from your local bakery, lottery tickets, etc., etc., etc.

PAPER INCENSE: Incense papers traditionally come from both France and Japan and are a beautiful inclusion in a letter; because they are coated with a fine dusting of scented powder, they infuse the entire envelope with a lovely, soft scent.

SACHETS: You know those flat white envelopes filled with lavender and rosemary that your grandmother stuck in her lingerie drawer? They still make them! And they mail like a dream.

EXTRA STICKY NOTES: Everyone can use them. I promise. Just tear a slender hunk off the pad on your desk and send away.

WASHI TAPE SAMPLES: Wrap some pretty reusable tape a few times around a slice of index card or cereal box cardboard and voilà! A mailable, thin roll of washi!

IRON-ON PATCHES: Turn your correspondent's Debbie Gibson mall-rat jean jacket fantasy into reality.

NEWSPAPER, CATALOG, OR MAGAZINE CLIPPINGS: Remember print media? I used to send catalog photos of slip dresses I wanted to buy or *Cosmopolitan* quizzes to my teenage pen pals, and I urge you to bring some deranged '90s découpage energy back to your correspondence by tucking an article or two into your next missive.

PRESSED LEAVES OR FLOWERS: How very Victorian of you! Sending flora never goes out of style. Buy yourself a book on the language of flowers and a plant press, and go to town.

A LOTTERY TICKET: Plus a humble request to split the winnings.

WITCHY ACCOUTREMENT: Tarot cards, moon charts, divination cards, spells, a heat-activated fish that predicts the future in your palm. Esoterica stores are *full* of flat delights to send.

POLAROIDS An instant camera is a must-have. Take generous snapshots of your city, your family, your pets, your daily commute, what you see out of your window while you write letters. Every picture you include saves you (at least) a thousand words of scribbling.

PLUS BOOKMARKS, PRESSED LEAVES OR FLOWERS, NOVELTY PAPER CLIPS, SHEET MASKS, SLEEP PATCHES, ZIT STICKERS, UNDER-EYE JELLIES, ROLLING PAPERS . . .

. . . *and many more.*

The sky—and whatever airmail carriers are able to transport through it—is the limit. Once you start looking for flat objects to slip into letters, you will begin to see them *everywhere*. I promise. Guard your wallets.

...but do not mail these!

Consider this me simply passing along a few hints I have gained through trial and error (and by reading the fine print on the USPS rules and regulations). These things *might* make it to their intended destination, and every now and then you have to take a risk just to see the reward. But, for the most part, if you want your letter to reach its recipient, leave these out (or use a box instead!):

COINS: I get it, mailing those leftover Euros seems like a glamorous and worldly idea. Sadly, most jangly, heavy metal objects do not tend to make it through the postal gauntlet.

MATCHBOOKS (WITH MATCHES STILL IN THEM): Technically illegal (though you can send certain enclosed matches via ground transportation).

PERFUME SAMPLES: A beautiful idea in theory, also legally forbidden in execution. You *can* mail alcohol-free perfume domestically, but if you don't want to chance it, just chuck the little vials in a bubble mailer or a box.

ANYTHING FRAGILE, BREAKABLE, OR POTENTIALLY LEAKY: If you think it can burst or crack in the mail, chances are . . . it will. Assume that your envelope will be squished, scrunched, dropped, and dragged along the way.

GLITTER OR CONFETTI: Mailing someone a "glitter bomb" is now technically a crime in many states. Opening your letter should not require a dust buster.

NO, THANK YOU!

Signature Sign-offs

It is lovely that, for both of us, there are echoes of the Beginnings. As always, I love you.

R.

Rachel Carson, in a letter
to Dorothy Freeman, 1958

✻

So long, old cabbage,

Zora

Zora Neale Hurston, in a letter
to Alain Locke, c. 1930

✻

All my love, you wicked,
grasping old bitch.

Noelie Wolie Polie

Noël Coward, in a letter
to Alexander Woollcott, 1933

✻

I love my country with
a wild volcanic love.

Thorny

Thornton Wilder, in a letter to Gertrude
Stein and Alice B. Toklas, 1936

Sexationally yours,

Mae West

Mae West, in a letter
to Alfred Kinsey, 1949

✻

Am Red beans and ricely yours,

Louis Armstrong

Louis Armstrong, in a letter
to Betty Jane Holder, 1952

✻

Kisses and please, burn my letters!

Tove Jansson, in a letter to
Eva Konikoff, 1952

✻

Yours, Affectionately

Jane Austen, in a letter to
her sister Cassandra, 1799

✻

Love always, in spite of myself!

M. F. K. Fisher, in a letter to
Lawrence Clark Powell, 1985

✻

L'amour toujours, you dolling goil,

Ursula

Ursula Nordstrom, in a letter
to Mary Rodgers, 1980

How to Press a Flower

Flower pressing, or the art of squeezing a flower until it becomes as flat and dry as warm ginger ale, has deep origins. Archaeologists have found still-preserved pressed flowers inside ancient Egyptian tombs and in the depths of the Paris catacombs. In Japan, the practice of *oshibana*, or the use of dried flowers as a colorful collage medium, dates back to the 1500s. But it was the Victorians who really pushed floral art to its limits; the flower press had a veritable vice grip on turn-of-the-twentieth-century crafters. Blooms—both dried and fresh—really had a moment in the Gilded Age.

Floriography, the study of the secret meanings of flowers and plants (roses for love, periwinkles for friendship, lavender for distrust, etc.), was a centuries-old practice that became so newly trendy in the late 1800s that many women walked around with nubby floral dictionaries tucked under their arms as accessories. Kate Greenaway's 1884 bestseller, *The Language of Flowers*, was so popular that it kicked off a petalmania that did not abate for decades. There were flower trading cards, flower identification guides, flower growing manuals, and famous flower gardens that became tourist destinations. People decorated their homes with big buckets of roses and bedside nosegays; men pinned blossoms to their lapels. And flower pressing—a way to savor a flower far past its expiration date—became a regular weekend pastime, particularly for letter writers. Tucking a dried flower into a letter was a way to send a hidden message while also celebrating the ephemerality of the botanical world.

The practice has fallen somewhat out of favor in the past century, except among the types of women who loved reading Frances Hodgson Burnett books as a child and who still own a proper tea set. Sure, you may have dried out your prom corsage for safekeeping or smashed a daisy or two between the pages of an old book. You may have even owned one of those flower presses made out of two pieces of cheap wood and some

basic screws that they sell in the gift shops of natural history museums. (You are reading this book, after all.) But for most people, flower pressing is more of an eccentric amusement than a typical Sunday afternoon activity. It is up to you as a letter writer to revive it as a regular practice. Flowers are still as weird and worth exalting as they were when the Victorians were fainting over them. All you need are a few stems from the bodega and some basic materials to bring it all back.

I am no flower-pressing expert—for this I turned to Lacie RZ Porta, who owns a business in Greenpoint, Brooklyn, called Framed Florals. Porta shares a sweet-smelling office inside an industrial warehouse with a vintage clothing seller and a professional florist, and their little collective has become a kind of one-stop shop for the in-the-know bride (first, you buy a gorgeous lace dress from the 1960s, then, you get a wildflower bouquet bursting with ranunculus and larkspur, and, lastly, you have it dried for posterity. Voilà!).

Porta's work is gorgeous. She presses wedding bouquets and anniversary flowers and prizewinning roses and aromatic herbs and then arranges the dried petals and leaves into delicate compositions between panes of glass. She makes her own wooden frames by hand. Her studio smells like dried lavender and eucalyptus and crushed juniper berries, and contains dozens of stacks of handmade wooden presses that are slowly curing petals and plants over a number of weeks and months. A stream of sunlight hits her desk in the afternoons, lending the room a pink, hazy glow. You can understand why a person might want to change their entire life to do this—and that is exactly what Porta did.

In 2015, when she got married, she was working as a preschool teacher. She loved her wedding arrangements so much that she wanted to save them, and remembered that, as a girl, she used to preserve flowers by tucking them into old books. This is exactly what she did with her bridal bouquet—and it is how she recommends that budding amateurs get started. You don't need a massive flower press or professional equipment. Porta now presses flowers full time and has more business than she can take on—as she walked me through her studio, holding up purple pansy leaves and dried rosemary sprigs with surgical tweezers, she gave me a quick lesson in Flower Pressing 101. And now . . . I pass that lesson on to you.

Flower Pressing 101

COURTESY OF LACIE RZ PORTA OF FRAMED FLORALS

1. **CHOOSE FRESH FLOWERS, HERBS, AND LEAVES THAT WILL PRESS WELL.** Flower pressing is essentially a process of drying out natural materials before they have time to get mushy or rotten, so it is best to pick fresh flowers (if they are already wilting, it's too late!) with thin, wispy petals that can press down flat. Still, Porta notes, any plant matter could work . . . if you take it apart. Roses or sunflowers, for example, do not press well if you keep the heads intact, but if you pluck off and dry individual petals, they work like a charm. "The more moist and the more dense a flower is, the harder it's going to pass and the longer the process," Porta says. "A lot of greenery, like jasmine and eucalyptus, will press really nicely because they don't hold a ton of moisture."

2. **FIND A LARGE OLD BOOK (OR JOURNAL) WITH MATTE PAGES—AND SOME CONSTRUCTION PAPER.** Porta suggests finding a book you are not too attached to—flower pressing is likely to stain and warp the pages. She likes to use blank journals. The more matte the paper, the better. If you are worried about ruining the book at all, Porta suggests inserting a few pieces of construction paper into the book before you begin. Avoid using paper towels or rough butcher paper, Porta says, as "They will leave textured markings behind on the flower."

3. **LAY OUT YOUR PETALS AND PLANT ON ONE PAGE (DON'T OVERLAP THEM!).** Use more than one book if you need to. Do not use multiple pages from the same book to press several plants—they risk seeping into each other or slowing down the drying process.

4. **CLOSE THE BOOK AND WRAP TIGHTLY WITH RUBBER BANDS.** Then, put a heavy stack of other books on top. Porta uses at least five coffee table books to weigh down her pressings. If you are attempting to press a thicker specimen, like a thistle head or a seedpod, it can be done, but you will need to add a lot of extra weight—the key is to get whatever is inside the book to be as flat as possible.

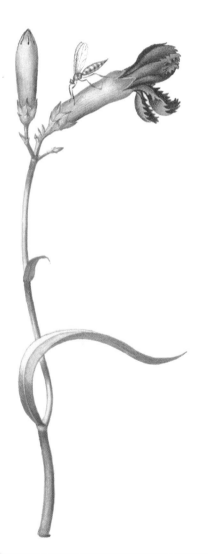

5. **NOW, YOU WAIT.** No peeking! This is the hard part. The more you open up the book to check the progress, the more you risk tearing or damaging the flowers as they are being transformed. Porta suggests checking up on your flowers once a week. Most flowers will take between three and four weeks to fully bake. Porta suggests "changing the paper out every week so that the flowers have a fresh, dry surface to rest on." For very juicy petals, she adds, you may have to change out the paper more frequently. You'll know the flower is done, Porta says, when it is "dry to the touch and lifts off the paper without sticking." Porta recommends using tweezers to handle the finished project. Most pressed petals are very fragile!

6. **EXPECT A BIT OF FADING, COLOR-MORPHING, OR SHRINKAGE.** Some flower preservationists use color-enhancing dyes to maintain the original vivid hues of their blossoms, but Porta chooses to go au naturel. "It's really a process of trial and error," Porta says. "The fun part is the surprise. Some leaves dry totally transparent, like vellum paper. Others turn into crinkle chips. Flowers that were purple turn blue, or even black."

7. **STORE YOUR WORK!** Porta, who keeps thousands of pressed flowers in her studio, stores hers on sheets of wax paper layered into airtight plastic tubs. She says that if you are just a hobbyist, however, you can keep your pressed flowers stored in the book you used, or in waxed glassine envelopes. You can also frame your flowers, ensuring they will officially last forever—or call a professional like Porta to frame them for you!

8. **DO IT AGAIN!** Every $8 bouquet from the bodega is a chance to fill more books with flora. You will know you are really a nouveau Victorian when you open a random novel from your shelf and a dried lily petal you did not even remember putting there falls out.

HOT TIP

Tuck your dried blooms into a letter!
Extra points if you include their hidden meanings.

ONION SKIN PAPER

In everyday life-at least in these times-one finds very little use for onion skin paper. It is whisper thin, prone to tearing and crinkling, and if you put it in a laser printer, it turns into shredded wheat and might just break the printer entirely. But in letter writing . . . it is fair game. In fact, onion skin paper-which is not, to be clear, made out of vegetables, but so named for its delicate, featherweight qualities that give it the flimsy feel of an onion wrapper-had its heyday in the early twentieth century as an airmail hack. Because it weighs almost nothing, using it helped to lower the cost of correspondence-a real benefit during wartime or economic depression.

To qualify as onion skin, the paper traditionally must have a high cotton fiber content (though some onion skin paper is made with wood pulp; there is much spirited debate about this on the fiber arts community message boards). Most onion skin also has something called a "cockle finish," which is a technical term for paper that has been a little roughed up so that it puckers and ripples in places. This helps the paper hold onto typewriter ink, and it also makes onion skin paper oddly bleed-proof despite its fragile appearance. While the classic uses for onion skin paper-as the buffer between a sheet of regular paper and a carbon copy sheet in a typewriter, as a tracing guide in the old-school cel animation process, as a cheap method for storing copious archival documents, or as the material for mass-produced, long books like hotel Bibles-may seem antiquated, onion skin is poised to make a comeback.

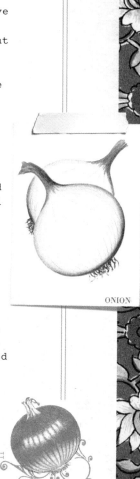

ONION

A few years ago, I ordered a ream of it online (you can find plenty of cheap options, and it lasts forever) and I pull it out whenever my other stationery starts to feel stale. It works best in a typewriter, but it also takes ink and pencil like a champ. There is nothing more satisfying than writing a long letter on onion skin paper, only to fold it up and find that the envelope feels empty. When someone opens that letter, they will get an unexpected jolt; all those words, and on paper that is no heavier than a butterfly wing. Writing on onion skin has a touch of whimsy to it, and a sense of humor: You are quite literally keeping it light.

In Praise of the Laminating Machine

Though I never felt the calling to become a schoolteacher, I always deeply coveted my teachers' regular access to laminating machines. For a time, I thought lamination was the most glamorous process on earth. What was once a humdrum piece of paper was now . . . enrobed in a gleamy, glossy shell. It was like putting an evening gown on an everyday document. In the third grade, I regularly skipped recess to stay inside as "class helper," which usually meant laminating flash cards and other floppy materials.

I was enchanted by the machine—which I now know is more or less a glorified flat iron that melts a sheet of cheap soft plastic and traps a flat object inside like a mosquito stuck in tree sap—and it felt like a far-off dream that I might grow up one day to have one of my own. Fast-forward to 2021, when I was looking for a way to preserve my flimsy vaccination card and I found that you could get your hands on a decent thermal laminator these days for less than the cost of a standard movie ticket. I've laminated vintage postcards that were about to disintegrate, sandwiched together découpaged collages, and preserved dried flowers and herbs. Channel your inner class helper and try it for yourself. My favorite laminating project is making matchbookmarks—see my method on page 59.

How to Make a Matchbookmark

At the beginning of every year, I order a box of custom matchbooks online (they always bear the same message: "Set [insert year here] on fire. xoxo Rachel"). I give them out at dinner parties and keep extras in my bag to give to friends and colleagues (and sometimes strangers I pass who ask if I have a light). I tuck them into care packages and bubble mailers (and, yes, even into envelopes sometimes if they are padded enough and not headed to an international location; you have to flirt with danger to feel alive). But mine are not the only matchbooks I keep lying around; I am a collector. I rarely leave a restaurant without checking to see if they have matches at the front desk. I love that they are such compact distillations of graphic design and personality.

During the pandemic, bored and scrolling, I discovered the world of vintage matchbook sellers on eBay. One lot of vintage New York matchbooks I ordered was so large that the seller had to pack them in a trash bag. I did not know, at first, *why* I was ordering hundreds of matchbooks or what I wanted to do with them, only that I had to have them. I found that most of the matchbooks I ordered were either missing their insides or the matches were so old that they turned to dust if you tried to strike them. Then, one day, I came across a matchbook from a defunct New York diner that I knew one of my regular correspondents—a woman who used to live in New York City in the 1980s but had since moved away—would appreciate, and I decided to run it through the laminating machine to preserve it further. The matchbookmark was born.

When I posted about my ad hoc crafting project online, my DMs flooded with requests from people looking for a specific matchbook (Did I have their father's favorite Italian eatery? Anything kitschy from Las Vegas or London? Anything tiki drink–themed?), and for one feverish month, I made hundreds of matchbookmarks to send out to strangers. While I quickly burned out on making bookmarks on demand, I still set aside a few Sunday afternoons per season to zone out and make a few dozen to keep in a cigar box near my desk, for when a letter demands a little extra spark.

THE MATCHBOOKMARK METHOD
A la Rachel

1. **SELECT A MATCHBOOK!** The generic, folded, 21-strike or 30-strike versions work best.

2. **REMOVE ANY MATCHES.** You can usually tear off the bottom of the book, where the matches are attached, in one firm yank—or, if you are a perfectionist, you can cleanly cut them off. You can also snip off the striking strip—it will be bulky in the laminator.

3. **FLATTEN YOUR MATCHBOOK.** To smooth out any serious creases, leave the flattened, stretched-out matchbook under a heavy tome or a cast-iron pot for a night.

4. **CHOOSE YOUR BACKING PAPER, IF USING.** Some matchbooks have slogans or secret messages printed on the inside that you will want to showcase; if yours is plain, gussy it up a bit by adding a backing. I will attach a swatch of old wallpaper or a page from a discount art book to the matchbook using thin, double-sided artist's tape.

5. **LAMINATE!** I suggest preparing several matchbooks at a time so you can fill up an entire laminating sheet with them. Press, melt, cut, and there you have it!

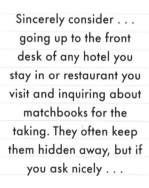

Sincerely consider . . . going up to the front desk of any hotel you stay in or restaurant you visit and inquiring about matchbooks for the taking. They often keep them hidden away, but if you ask nicely . . .

Every Artist Needs Her Tools

- A proper pen (ballpoint, fountain, or even a quill . . .)

- A calligraphy pen and an inkwell (along with one bottle of basic, black calligrapher's ink and one of watery walnut ink, for when you are feeling fancy)

- Good-quality writing paper that can stand up to wet fountain-pen ink

- A typewriter

- A shoebox full of blank, miscellaneous postcards

- Stamps galore!

- Scraps of random paper (origami, newsprint, musical scores, Playbills, magazine tear-outs, etc.)

- Return address labels or a custom address stamp

- Rubber stamps and at least one pad of archival-grade stamp ink

- Sticker books, rolls, and sheets

- Double-sided tape and/ or washi tape for sealing and decorating envelopes

- Good crafting scissors (and maybe novelty scissors for scalloped or zigzag edges)

- A hot glue gun

- A letter opener (eBay is a treasure trove for vintage brass ones!)

- A lap desk for answering correspondence from your bed or the couch

- A laminating machine

- A bottle of perfume for scenting your paper

- Sealing wax and a wax seal (not an essential, per se, but nice to have on hand)

- A Polaroid camera for including a snapshot of your day

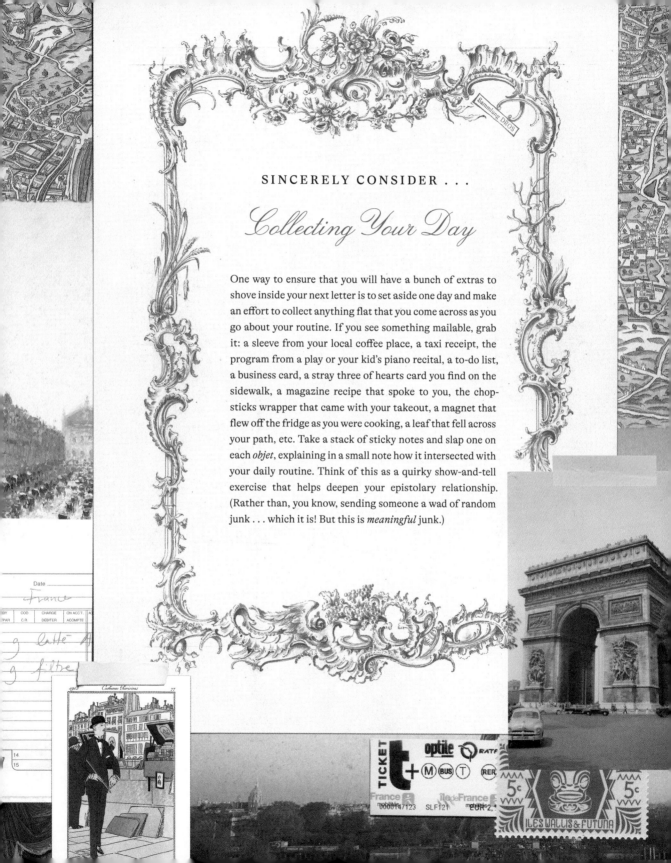

SINCERELY CONSIDER . . .

Collecting Your Day

One way to ensure that you will have a bunch of extras to shove inside your next letter is to set aside one day and make an effort to collect anything flat that you come across as you go about your routine. If you see something mailable, grab it: a sleeve from your local coffee place, a taxi receipt, the program from a play or your kid's piano recital, a to-do list, a business card, a stray three of hearts card you find on the sidewalk, a magazine recipe that spoke to you, the chopsticks wrapper that came with your takeout, a magnet that flew off the fridge as you were cooking, a leaf that fell across your path, etc. Take a stack of sticky notes and slap one on each *objet*, explaining in a small note how it intersected with your daily routine. Think of this as a quirky show-and-tell exercise that helps deepen your epistolary relationship. (Rather than, you know, sending someone a wad of random junk . . . which it is! But this is *meaningful* junk.)

To Perfume or Not Perfume?

Atomizer—Spray.

The scented letter has been a subject of pungent debate for over a century; the Victorians were constantly arguing about whether or not perfuming your paper, which was all the rage at the time, was a welcome gilding or a noxious annoyance. In an issue of *Good Housekeeping* from 1889, a manners expert named Anna Sawyer addressed the issue directly in her column "The Etiquette of Correspondence":

The question is often asked if the use of perfumed paper is allowable. There can be no objection to it in social notes but the odor should be of the most delicate nature. A faint touch of orris is perhaps best, and heliotrope or violet is pleasant, but the heavier odors, as musk, or patchouli are vulgar in the extreme.

Orris, or the fatty root of the iris flower that looks like a knob of ginger and smells like steamy basmati rice and old books and fusty flower petals fried in coconut oil, does smell lovely, as Sawyer suggests, when applied to paper. The same goes for heliotrope flowers, small purple blooms that sigh off their scent through a fussy process called "enfleurage." Heliotrope essence has the soapy cleanliness of cotton blossoms with an almost almondy undertone, like the sweet orgeat syrup that street vendors in Italy glug into soda water. Violet, which Sawyer also mentions in her column, was a star ingredient in most late-nineteenth-century perfumes—the corseted set went absolutely mad for the smell of talc mixed with a dewy garden (if you've ever had chalky violette pastille candy, you have tapped directly into Victorian eros). What these "pleasant" letter scents have in common, besides being sweet and floral, is that they have a powdery undertone that happens to cling perfectly to paper. Powder releases its scent in small, discreet puffs, so that the reader rarely experiences olfactory overload. Sawyer might have been onto something when she said to avoid musk and patchouli, though I love both notes and do not find them the least bit vulgar; just know that animalic and woody notes tend to go funky on paper and grow sour and strong over time, like a tea bag left to steep too long.

But the question remains: Should you perfume your letters to begin with? The scented note has a romantic aura around it (see the scene from *Grease* in which Sandy asks to borrow a piece of stationery from Marty, and Marty coats the paper generously with perfume), but it can be controversial. In *Legally Blonde*, we see Elle Woods hand a law professor her resume, pink and liberally spritzed with fragrance. This is a kind of visual punch line—we are supposed to believe that Elle is the kind of prissy ditz who brings lip gloss to a professional knife fight and who has no place being a lawyer—but also it is Elle's attention to aesthetic details that ends up winning over critics. Is Elle's perfumed note a sign of her frivolity or is it, as she argues, "a little something extra" that puts her ahead of the pack?

When I began writing lots of letters, I liberally scented them; I write about fragrance often and collect perfume, so it felt very on-brand. But then I started to get subtle hints that the hints of rose and jasmine I had been infusing my paper with were not so subtle. One of my pen pals gently wrote to me about her migraines that were triggered by scents without ever directly asking me to lay off the spritzing—but I got the message. While Anna Sawyer writes that "There can be no objection to it in social notes," the truth is that not everyone likes being bombarded with fumes while opening the mail. That said, if you do want to scent your letters, there are elegant ways to go about it.

THE PROPER WAY TO SPRITZ A LETTER

1. **ASK BEFORE SCENTING:** What you lose in the element of surprise, you gain the confidence that you aren't mailing someone an unwanted headache. Those with allergies or olfactory sensitivities will thank you for asking first.

2. **SCENT BEFORE WRITING:** You should always spray your paper/envelope interior with perfume (or a mixture of essential oil and water in a spray bottle) before you begin writing, and allow it to dry completely before you put down a single word. Otherwise, you will smear your ink.

3. **INCLUDE A SEPARATE SCENT SWATCH:** One way to get scent into your letters without touching your stationery (or causing your ink to bleed) is to spray perfume on a tissue or a piece of absorbent blotting paper and tuck it into your letter.

4. **"MARINATE" YOUR STATIONERY:** Place your stationery in an airtight box with a highly scented item like cinnamon sticks, whole coffee beans, or lavender for a week or two. The paper will emerge from the box with a subtle whisper of its scented surroundings.

5. **USE SCENTED INK:** The Parisian fountain pen ink purveyor Jacques Herbin, which has been in business since 1670, makes a line of beautiful, scented ink that contains notes like lime, vetiver, moss, tobacco, honey, fresh hay, and orange blossom. Scented ink is the faintest way to add scent to a letter (you can barely smell it once it dries), but it is fun to use and feels like a mischievous little tryst between you and the page.

HOW TO WRITE A LETTER ABOUT YOUR DREAMS

Dreams are, in many ways, like body aches: They are highly personal, extremely vivid when you are experiencing them, and nobody else (except, perhaps, a qualified professional) really likes to hear about them. The half-life of a good dream is incredibly short; from the moment you wake up, it begins to ferment, and talking about it only hastens the process. Nothing kills a tranquil morning vibe like rolling over and telling the person in bed next to you that you just had *the most incredible dream* and it involved a carnival barker and a boa constrictor and also, somehow, your fourth-grade bully and also Orson Welles eating a steak? A Freudian analyst might be able to untangle all of this, but you'd have to pay them at least $300 an hour. If you talk too much about dreams, you can start to sound maudlin—even the usually precise and restrained writer Iris Murdoch sounded meandering when writing to a friend about dreams in a letter in 1963:

> Do you feel it is very kind of people to dream about you? I always feel rather grateful if I learn I have been in someone's dream. Metaphysical query: is one morally responsible for what one does in other people's dreams?

This all said, dreams do have a place in letter-writing—perhaps letters are the best place for one's dreams to land. You can dissect and untangle the symbols and secret meanings, the anxieties and fears that have bubbled up from your subconscious. In writing, dream-talk can shift from tedious to engrossing.

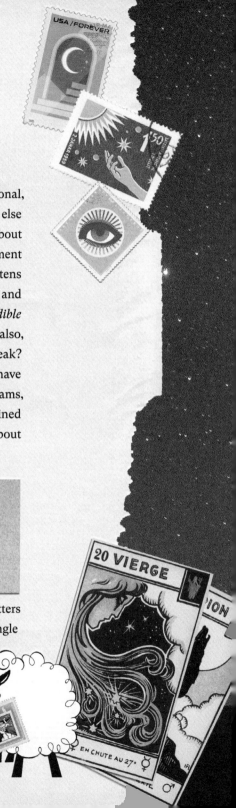

Take, for example, the writer and feminist thinker Simone de Beauvoir. She would write to her "sweet little one" (as she was known to nickname her partner, Jean-Paul Sartre; she liked to sign her letters to him as "Your Charming Beaver") about the wild meanderings of her snoozing mind. She wrote of one dream she had at her grandmother's house, after a robust meal of sausages, where she imagined Sartre trying to murder her while wearing a soldier's uniform, before he relented and let her softly stroke his hair. She wrote that she woke up furious; how could he have tried to kill her? And in uniform, no less!

All of the details de Beauvoir recounts, taken separately, are the banal stuff of standard REM hallucinations, perhaps brought on by eating fatty meat products too close to bedtime. But taken altogether, there is a charming snowball effect to her words. She gives away detail beneath the details—she is such an uncompromising thinker that she was angry at herself mid-dream for finding her unconscious mind embroiled in a cliché.

In a letter, writing about your dreams can be a shortcut to writing about yourself, as long as you are willing to be specific and unmerciful about what they might mean. So, try it: For a week, keep a notebook near your bed, and write down what you dreamt about immediately upon waking. Be as meticulous as you can, knowing that you are trying to capture sand falling through a sieve. In mere moments, it will be gone. Get yourself a copy of Stearn Robinson and Tom Corbett's 1974 bestseller *The Dreamer's Dictionary* (it is a bit dated in parts, but has a funky, earthy quality that makes it more or less timeless). Write someone a letter at the end of the week about what you dreamed about, and what you think it reveals about what's simmering underneath the surface; there is always something you have been meaning to write about but don't have the words yet to describe. Let your dreams do the work for you.

Try curating your own letter-writing playlists to fit certain moods. This one is my homage to the way it feels to stare out of a cab window as you are going over a bridge alone after a hectic night; but you can make yours about anything. Make a playlist of songs with flowers in the title; or one full of power ballads, or a mix of opera arias or film scores or dance bops that really hype you up. Write your letter to it, then send your pen pal a link to listen to it. An immersive soundtrack!

A LATE NIGHT LETTER-WRITING PLAYLIST

01. IS THAT ALL THERE IS?"—Peggy Lee

02. "I THOUGHT OF YOU LAST NIGHT"—Jeri Southern

03. "WALK ON BY"—Dionne Warwick

04. "SUDDENLY THERE'S A VALLEY"—Petula Clark

05. "THE FIRST TIME EVER I SAW YOUR FACE"—Roberta Flack

06. "L'ETANG"—Blossom Dearie

07. "I CRY BY NIGHT"—Kay Starr

08. "I WISH YOU LOVE"—Nancy Wilson

09. "LILAC WINE"—Helen Merrill

10. "BEWITCHED, BOTHERED, AND BEWILDERED"—Ella Fitzgerald

11. "CRY ME A RIVER"—Julie London

12. "THE MAN I LOVE"—Billie Holiday

13. "STORMY WEATHER"—Etta James

14. "TIME AFTER TIME"—Margaret Whiting

15. "SOMETHING COOL"—June Christy

16. "SEPTEMBER SONG"—Sarah Vaughan

17. "I NEED YOUR LOVE SO BAD"—Irma Thomas

18. "BLUE SKIES"—Maxine Sullivan

19. "SMOKE GETS IN YOUR EYES"—Eartha Kitt

20. "IT'LL TAKE A LONG TIME"—Sandy Denny

THIS IS JUST ONE OF MANY MIXES I'VE MADE—USE IT AS AN INSPIRATION TO SET YOUR OWN VIBE.

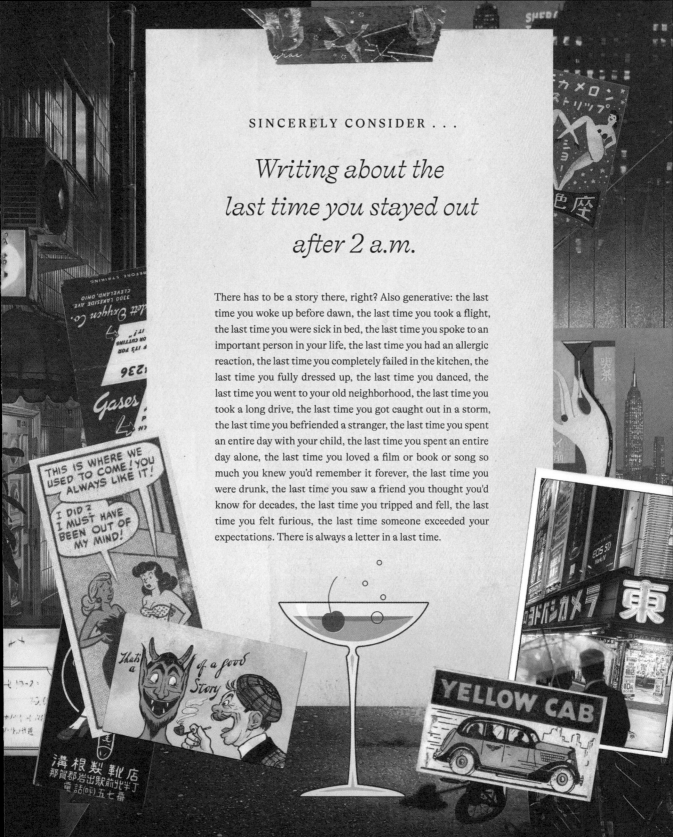

Writing about the last time you stayed out after 2 a.m.

There has to be a story there, right? Also generative: the last time you woke up before dawn, the last time you took a flight, the last time you were sick in bed, the last time you spoke to an important person in your life, the last time you had an allergic reaction, the last time you completely failed in the kitchen, the last time you fully dressed up, the last time you danced, the last time you went to your old neighborhood, the last time you took a long drive, the last time you got caught out in a storm, the last time you befriended a stranger, the last time you spent an entire day with your child, the last time you spent an entire day alone, the last time you loved a film or book or song so much you knew you'd remember it forever, the last time you were drunk, the last time you saw a friend you thought you'd know for decades, the last time you tripped and fell, the last time you felt furious, the last time someone exceeded your expectations. There is always a letter in a last time.

SINCERELY CONSIDER . . .

Griffin and Sabine

As long as we are on the subject of dreams, one of the dreamiest things you can do for yourself as a letter enthusiast is to order a copy of Nick Bantock's novel, *Griffin and Sabine: An Extraordinary Correspondence.* The book, when it came out in 1991, was a surprise bestseller—who would have thought that a set of imaginary letters between two strangers written by an unknown author living on a small island off the coast of Vancouver would be a smash?

Bantock was a freelance illustrator who worked on book covers before setting out to create something of sui generis, and what he made was so deeply specific, and so deeply his own, that it ended up shooting the moon and tipping into something approaching universal appeal. At the time he wrote the first *Griffin and Sabine* book (eventually, he would write a trilogy), Bantock was living on Bowen Island, a misty, mysterious, sparsely inhabited place that is only 3.7 miles across at its widest point and that one must take a ferry to reach. Something about the strangeness of his surroundings must have put Bantock into a mystical state, because *Griffin and Sabine* seems to spring from that hazy netherworld between the conscious and the unconscious mind (Jungian scholars love it!).

The premise, in case you are new to it, is that Griffin Moss, a grumpy stationery designer living in London, receives

Hello!

"*Sabine,*

Thank you for your exotic postcard. Forgive me if it's a memory lapse on my part, but should I know you?"

—from *Griffin and Sabine*

a postcard out of the blue from a woman who calls herself Sabine Strohem and says she lives in the Sicmon Islands in the South Pacific. Everything about this correspondence feels fishy and unreal, at least at first; there are no Sicmon Islands (Bantock invented them), and furthermore, Sabine claims to be clairvoyant and to be able to read Griffin's mind from miles away. The two keep writing back and forth, but Griffin soon believes that he is losing his grip on reality; is Sabine just a figment of his imagination, a dream he conjured up out of his solitude? She seems too magical to be true, and he ends up rebuffing her in a letter, only to have her write back with increased urgency. She insists that she is not only alive, but that the two have a cosmic connection that cannot be denied. The aspect of the book that made it so remarkable was its formatting—Bantock included full, pull-out letters (much like the one at the beginning of this book; I credit him with the inspiration) and otherworldly postcards and original stamps that he designed himself. The pleasure of the book—as with actual letters—is its tactility; you can touch, unfold, open the envelopes for yourself. It's like a pop-up book for adults. The book replicates a real correspondence that also feels eerily unfamiliar, like a secret archive that you have stumbled onto in a stranger's attic. Reading it feels like entering an off-kilter dimension where the rules of our world don't quite make sense. To me, it remains the most accurate depiction of the bubble inhabited by two people when the letters they write attain escape velocity and start to form their own language. *Griffin and Sabine* was the book that made me want to write letters consistently and it still has that effect on me. I recommend keeping it near your desk to flip through whenever your letters feel stale—it will remind you of how fantastical and surreal this practice can be.

Creating a Letter-Writing Ritual

(OR THE IMPORTANCE OF THE CORRESPONDENCE HOUR)

JOHANNES VERMEER,
"A LADY WRITING." C. 1665

In nearly every major classical art museum, you will find at least one *Portrait of a Woman Writing a Letter*—for a time, it was a very robust painting genre. One of my favorites, Johannes Vermeer's *A Lady Writing*, from 1665, sits in the National Gallery in London and shows a young woman wearing huge pearl earrings and an entire notions box worth of ribbons in her hair, along with a highly impractical plush jacket with speckled-fur trimmings that is the color of lemon meringue pie. She sits at a table covered in a bright blue cloth and holds a quill lightly in her hand. Her stare is focused not on her paper, but on the voyeur, as if to say, "Oh, this? This is my letter-writing time. *I dare you to watch.*"

Vermeer was not the only artist drawn to the subject of women writing—other Dutch painters like Gerard der Bosch were drawn to the subject in the seventeenth century, and, in the eighteenth century, the Japanese painter Kaigetsudō Doshin made his famous painting *Courtesan Writing a Letter*, which now sits in the Metropolitan Museum's permanent collection (courtesans writing was a prominent motif among Ukiyo-e painters during this time).

In the Victorian era, both the Impressionists and the Realists took up the tradition, painting sumptuous portraits of women at their desks, usually while wearing corsets, as in Albert Edelfelt's *Lady Writing a Letter* from 1887.

SUZUKI HARUNOBU
"THE COURTESAN KASUGANO
WRITING A LETTER." C. 1765

ALBERT EDELFELT.
"LADY WRITING A LETTER," 1887

There is certainly a pervasive male gaze in all of these portraits (the way Edelfelt painted the sunlight hitting the woman's décolletage as she scribbles, for example) and perhaps a bit of condescension—for centuries, women weren't really encouraged to write books or other such ambitious projects (those who managed to publish fought tooth and nail for the opportunity). As such, the only deeply engaged writing that any portrait artist saw women doing regularly was writing letters; it was seen as a cute hobby, a frivolous-but-necessary domestic skill, and a side hustle for the woman of the house (or for an industrious courtesan with time to kill). Many women handled the correspondence duties for the family, keeping track of coming visitors and news from far-flung friends and any pressing requests that arrived via mail. As such, women's letters smoothed over family squabbles, paved the way for their children's education, and otherwise kept the household connected to the outside world (and with all the hottest gossip of the day). If you see a woman writing in a painting from before 1900, she is almost certainly writing a letter, and she is almost certainly holding her family's social life together by doing it.

Men wrote letters, too, of course—and sometimes the act was even the subject of a portrait, as in Dutch master Gabriel Metsu's *Man Writing a Letter*, which hangs in the National Gallery of Ireland—but the act wasn't as doted upon or captured so fervently in art. Perhaps the artists who devoted themselves to painting women writing were trying to diminish their subjects—oh look, the ladies are doing their *little letters* again—but perhaps they were also trying, in some way, to dignify the practice and raise it to the level of

CAMILLE COROT,
"THE LETTER," C. 1865

an artistic preoccupation. I love looking at paintings of women at their desks—even if they look terribly uncomfortable trying to hunch over a bottle of ink in a boned corset—because, in them, I see the effort and the hours spent scratching nib to paper. And I see the work that goes into developing a daily practice.

When letters were still the most vital way for human beings to communicate over long distances, people would set aside regular times of day to reply to the post. The "correspondence hour," as it was sometimes known, was a sacred time when a person could sit alone and write without distraction. Now, our lives are overflowing with distraction. I'm not here to tell you to throw your phone into the sea, but I am here to tell you that you might want to consider locking it in a drawer for an hour during whatever time of the week you can spare to turn to your stack of mail.

Make your own correspondence hour, with your own eccentric rules, and stick to them. Make a cocktail or a mint lemonade or a strong espresso. Put on a favorite robe (or sweater, or lemon meringue jacket—your house, your rules). Light a specific candle. Sit down at your dining table or at your desk or in your favorite chair with a lap desk (a product I thought I'd never own until I started writing letters— now I cannot imagine life without one). Fill your fountain pen with good ink. Put on a dedicated soundtrack for the occasion. If anyone tries to bother you, simply tell them, "I am tending to my correspondence." Be defiant about this time. Channel a Dutch woman, scribbling away in a sunbeam. Maybe someone will paint you.

Jan Vermeer van Delft

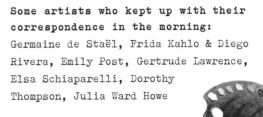

Some artists who kept up with their correspondence in the morning:
Germaine de Staël, Frida Kahlo & Diego Rivera, Emily Post, Gertrude Lawrence, Elsa Schiaparelli, Dorothy Thompson, Julia Ward Howe

(Or how to arrange a letter-writing desk)

PAR avion

THE DESK

OPEN LATE

HOW TO WRITE
A LETTER FROM ABROAD

(OR, REALLY, FROM ANYWHERE)

The "letter home" is a time-honored tradition, though it is one that has mostly been lost. These days, there are other, more immediate ways to broadcast your travels around the world, to the world. Why send a telegram when there is Instagram? Why spend the time to tell one person about your week in Santorini when you can make one thousand people jealous of your ouzo-drinking-at-sunset with a single click? I'm not going to pry the phone out of your hands while you are on a trip (I can barely pry it from my own), but simply want to suggest, perhaps, that you put it down every now and then, and steal a few minutes from your wanderings to sit down and write a letter to someone back home. It will put you in a grand lineage of letter writers who sent delightful dispatches from far away in an attempt to both make sense of their surroundings and to whisk the receiver along, however briefly, as a kind of imaginary travel companion.

It is worth acknowledging that, nowadays, a letter you send from abroad might get home long after you do. It's not an efficient medium. In the days of the steamship, when it took two weeks to cross the Atlantic and another two weeks for a letter from the continent to get back home, people would wait for months to hear whether or not someone had safely arrived at a destination. A letter from across the sea was not just a hello, it was a lifeline—it was the best way to inform your anxious mother that you had at last arrived in Tokyo, or had made it to New York without catching cholera or scurvy. Gone are the days of pacing nervously for weeks to see if someone is still alive after an epic journey (and that's a good thing, blood pressure–wise), but I like to think of writing letters from wherever you are in the world as a no less insistent activity than it once was. You don't need to report that you didn't die along the way, but letter writing does reaffirm the fact that you are aware and attuned to the world as you are moving through it. I like to choose who I am going to write to before I take a trip—I recommend asking a few friends if you can have their addresses before you go and write them down in a notebook that you keep in your carry-on. It helps to know you are going to put your day into a letter, because it will get you in the habit of noticing details: the crackle of a baguette, the sound of a brass band on the street, the smell of briny fish, the oily surface of an ancient canal, the vivid colors of a fruit stand.

Your letters home need not be extensive or sprawling. The great food writer M. F. K. Fisher, who bounced back and forth regularly between California, Provence, and Switzerland, would often just send her friends lists of what she ate while traveling. In 1959, she wrote to her friend Eleanor Friede from Switzerland about a meal that consisted of "a box of salted wafers, 8 slices of salami, 3 Petits Suisses, half a large tube of cherry jam, and a lot of grapes." The poet Elizabeth Bishop, writing to her friend, the poet Marianne Moore, from Mexico City in 1942, simply noted what was going on outside her window. "They are celebrating the birthday of the Little Flower here for the last three days," she wrote. "Last night from my window I saw an amazing float going by . . . in the float stood six little girls in nightgowns of pale blue satin, and blue crowns, all laughing and having a wonderful time drinking Orange Crush out of bottles."

Yes, it can be a hassle to write letters on your vacation. But it can also *be* the vacation. There are adventures to be had in finding local stationers, in locating foreign stamps (Hint: Always ask someone at the front desk of your hotel), in navigating the vagaries of an unfamiliar postal system. There is no quicker way to get to know a place than to familiarize yourself with its bureaucratic institutions and postage pricing.

Also, here's a secret: You don't have to travel very far to write a letter home. You can sit in a new café that just opened down the block or get off at a subway stop far from your apartment. You can walk ten minutes in a direction you don't usually go and wind up under a tree you've never seen before. The letter that you write home has less to do with where you are physically and more to do with where you are mentally—which is to say, that you are open to a new experience, and you are open to sharing that experience with another person. If it has been a while since I've traveled, I will just tuck a box of stationery into a tote bag before I leave the apartment and jot down pieces of a letter as I run errands around the city. It's not as romantic as sending someone a note from Rome or Bangkok, but it makes an otherwise harried day feel a little more enchanted.

Postcrossing

So, you are now in possession of some postcards you love, you have the postage, you have a pen at the ready, and . . . you have nobody to send one to. You've sent them to all your friends and family and got one sad "Oh, that's nice, honey" response (if you got a response at all), and yet you are still yearning to fling these cards at people. Don't despair!

During the pandemic's first year, I stumbled across Postcrossing .com, a delightfully old-school website that launched out of Portugal in 2005. A student there named Paulo Magalhães was in the same predicament as most postcard enthusiasts: a lot of great cards to send and nobody to address them to. So he developed a site that allows anyone to sign up and start chucking postcards all over the world. The process itself is simple: You make an account and you get a stranger's address somewhere around the globe. Once you send your first card, someone else will get your address, and surprise cards will begin to show up from the likes of Germany, India, Japan, or Croatia.

I have gotten cards from tiny islands in the South Pacific and from central London, from a teacher in a corner of Finland where it is sunny nineteen hours a day and from an olive farmer in Greece. The whole thing feels a bit like a live-action Carmen Sandiego game; each postcard has a unique ID number that you write on the back and when your recipient receives the card, they enter the code into the website and a little map pops up illustrating the journey your card took. The site stores all of your postcards, both sent and received, on a gallery wall that you can wander through whenever you feel bored.

There are glitches, of course. The site's forum is a gossipy wonderland about the inefficiencies of the international mail system. Cards get lost (and they expire after being in the ether for sixty days) and there are weeks that go by when your mailbox will be empty. But I have found nothing more magical or addictive than participating in this global experiment, and it is a marvelous way to know that people will really appreciate that quirky card you found. In a time when the Internet is amplifying our disconnections, Postcrossing feels like a little miracle. Give it a whirl!

On Airmail

In 2007, the United States Postal Service discontinued its international sea mail program, meaning that currently, all letters that must cross a body of water make the journey via airplane. Gone are the days of ocean liners hauling mail bags across the Atlantic—these days, all international mail (at least that which originates in the United States) is technically airmail. As such, you are no longer required to write "Airmail" on the front of an envelope or put a "Par Avion" sticker on a letter (in postal lingo, these stickers are known as "airmail etiquette") if you want your correspondence to travel through the skies. But that doesn't mean you *can't* use airmail etiquettes—if anything, I encourage you to seek out a stash of them to use whenever you want to commune with the postal pioneers of the past.

Airmail—like aviation itself—has a dynamic history full of twists and turns. Those who study this history (also known as *aerophilatelists*) do not always agree on the moment when airmail officially began. Was it when people began tying letters to the legs of homing pigeons? Was it with the advent of balloon flight in the eighteenth century? (Many consider the first American airmail success to be a letter from George Washington that made its way from Philadelphia to New Jersey via hot air balloon.) The decade most commonly associated with the birth of modern airmail is the 1910s, when, in 1911, pilot Earle Ovington made the first official US Postal Service airmail flight in a Blériot monoplane. Ovington's flight from Garden City, New York, to the nearby town of Mineola only took about six minutes, but it kicked off a massive shift in the way people could communicate. Before airmail, a letter could take up to two weeks to cross the country (and several months if it was going abroad); suddenly the commute was cut down to as little as one or two days. We take this speed for granted now—I know that I grow impatient if a letter takes longer than a week to get anywhere on Earth—but I try to remember that it was, at one time, nearly miraculous.

AERIAL MAIL PERMANENT

THE AERIAL MAIL, operating 100 per cent perfect daily, is now a permanent service of the Post Office Department.

In the first five months of its operation it has performed more than 50,000 miles of service, has carried more than 2,000,000 letters, and has cut in half the time between Washington and New York.

A letter by aerial mail costs only 3 cents more than a letter sent by special delivery. By reason of the special treatment given, it is practically as speedy, under existing congestion, as the telegraph, more desirable because it has the privacy of a sealed communication, and more serviceable because it admits of inclosures.

OTTO PRAEGER,
Second Assistant Postmaster General.

If you ever find yourself yearning to learn more postal history (and believe me, it is a fascinating rabbit hole in which to spend a few insomniac nights), I encourage you to look up the period during World War I when many women pushed their way into aviation due to the shortage of domestic pilots. The first airmail pilots were in the US Army Air Service, but once the war began, the USPS moved to hire civilians—including women—to do the job. Amelia Earhart never technically worked for the postal service, though she often schlepped mailbags with her on her flights. The pilots Ruth Law and Katherine Stinson both became national airmail celebrities in the 1910s: In 1916, Law set a distance record of 700 miles, and in 1918, Stinson broke it by flying 783 miles between Chicago and New York in order to establish a new airmail route (Stinson technically crashed her plane two miles before reaching New York City and had to wait over a week for a new propeller blade, but once her plane was repaired she completed her run).

USE ZIP CODE

I am surprised there has not yet been a prestige television series about the dueling aviatrixes who raced to deliver the mail—both women had dazzling, high-flying careers and fairly dramatic endings. Law was forced into early retirement by a husband who no longer wanted her to fly, and suffered from a nervous breakdown in her forties due to her despair over missing the high altitude. Stinson quit the postal service late in World War I after a work dispute and moved to Europe to drive ambulances for the Red Cross; she got tuberculosis during her travels and moved to New Mexico to fill her lungs with dry air. She lived out the rest of her days in an adobe house, land-bound.

Airmail is now more of an aesthetic—the blue-and-red striped envelopes, the retro stickers—than it is a practical concern. The USPS, which once issued special "air mail stamps," now only produces reproductions as tribute (I am partial to the 2018 Forever stamp that features a Curtiss Jenny biplane). Still, it can be fun to tap into the airmail spirit, gussying your envelope up for an intercontinental adventure whenever you want to channel a time when people regularly risked their lives just to shave a few days off of a letter's arrival.

Aerial Mail Service

BETWEEN

New York, Philadelphia, & Washington

Daily, Except Sunday

Dependable and 100 Per Cent Perfect

COSTS only 3 cents per ounce more than Special-Delivery Service, and insures Special Treatment from the time of mailing to the time of delivery by fast messenger

SOUTHBOUND

Leave N. Y. 12.00 Noon   Arrive Phila. 1.10 P.M.
Leave Phila. 1.25 P. M.   Arrive Wash. 3.20 P.M.

NORTHBOUND

Leave Wash. 11.30 A. M.   Arrive Phila. 1.15 P.M.
Leave Phila. 1.30 P. M.   Arrive N. Y. 2.30 P.M.

WRITING ON
HOTEL STATIONERY

In a 1990 interview with the *Paris Review*, the poet Maya Angelou revealed that renting hotel rooms was a crucial and cherished aspect of her writing process. "I have kept a hotel room in every town I've ever lived in. I rent a hotel room for a few months, leave my home at six, and try to be at work by six-thirty," she said. "I insist that all things are taken off the walls. I don't want anything in there. I go into the room and I feel as if all my beliefs are suspended. Nothing holds me to anything. No milkmaids, no flowers, nothing. I just want to feel and then when I start to work I'll remember."

The idea of a hotel room of one's own—a transitory, transformative space for feeling, disconnected from time or obligations—is endlessly romantic as a form of purposeful departure and even creative rebellion. This is especially true for women writers, who historically have had to take tangible and often dramatic steps to disconnect from the rhythms of daily responsibility. Carving out a quiet space to drape oneself across a bed with crisp linens and a slice of cheesecake only a phone call away is a luxury, but it can also be a lifeline. Also: Hotels have the best stationery.

You don't have to book a hotel room for months at a time to channel the pleasures of scrawling notes on kitschy letterhead in a king-size bed that is not your own, staring out on a view you will never see again. In fact, many hotels no longer provide notepads or pens (sigh!) as a concession to the digital age. This is where Etsy or eBay come in: Vintage hotel paper is a staple of online flea markets, and there is more or less an endless variety to collect.

WALDORF-ASTORIA ÷ NEW YORK

You can get ornate, buttery envelopes from grand old hotels like the Waldorf-Astoria or the Plaza or the Ritz Paris on the Place Vendôme. You can seek out tacky, lounge lizard–esque notepads from Route 66 motels. You can source rustic paper with line drawings of oak trees and mountains from popular mid-century ski lodges. There is hot-pink stationery from Florida beachcomber inns, chintzy floral paper from rural bed-and-breakfasts, and faded postcards from resorts halfway across the world, featuring castles and palm trees and gluttonous buffet tables overflowing with lobster and cake. There are always treasures to find—and for cheap—if you open enough tabs.

The key: Look for something that delights you just enough that you don't mind letting it go. The whole point of hotel stationery is that it should be transient. It wants to be in motion. Hotels can be havens—especially for women like Angelou who were able to go there and find enough peace to go wild—but they are also ephemeral. At some point, you have to check out. Someone else will arrive in search of the promise of refuge and fresh sheets. All you can do is keep moving, too, and keep a chronicle of where you have been. Go out and find your own set of fresh sheets (of stationery!) and write someone a letter about the last time you had a solo adventure. Make yourself a giant pot of coffee and pretend you ordered room service. Put on your fluffiest robe. Write about all the places you yearn to go, even if getting there seems impossible. Think about what you could do if nothing held you to anything. No milkmaids, no flowers. Just paper from a strange room, ready to get to the next place.

TERMINUS - 108. RUE ST-LAZARE - PARIS

A FEW IDEAS FOR
WRITING WHILE AWAY

When in doubt, send a list! You don't have to write in complete, fluttery paragraphs when sending a letter back home from another place. If anything, lists are the quickest way to transmit the sensory pleasures of being elsewhere. So, here are a few inspirations for ways to compose a list on the back of a postcard.

Sit on a bench for an hour and write down (or draw!) the most eccentric outfits you see.

SIT AT A CAFÉ AND EAVESDROP ON LOCAL CONVERSATIONS.

Write down the five most interesting phrases you overhear in between every beverage you consume.

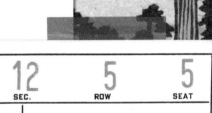

ATTEND SOME KIND OF PERFORMANCE—A THEATER PRODUCTION, A MUSICAL GIG AT A CAFE, A DANCE PERFORMANCE— AND WRITE IN A MINI-DISPATCH ABOUT THE PERFORMERS.

Strike up a conversation with a barista at a coffee shop. Whether it goes anywhere or not, write about your new friend.

CHOCOLAT EXPRESS
LE MEILLEUR

Try at least five different local desserts. Report back in extreme detail.

Buy a round-trip train ticket to somewhere an hour away. Don't make a plan. Keep notes throughout the excursion, and narrate the entire day in a letter.

If you can dream it, you can find it printed on a postcard and for sale on eBay. But online shopping is a sucker's market compared to the postcard finds you can score at flea markets and yard sales, where sellers are often happy to part with hundreds of postcards for whatever price you care to haggle. Often flea market sellers will have boxes full of used postcards, which are fun from an archival/voyeuristic perspective, but also totally reusable. Just slap a fresh sheet of paper on the back with a glue stick, cut to size, and voilà! Fresh postcard with a bonus hidden message underneath!

Tuck away into a local bookshop for a few hours. Draw some of your favorite nooks and describe the architecture and atmosphere to bring your reader into the shop with you.

If you are near an ocean or another body of water, describe the ways it changes colors and textures throughout the day.

Go to a grocery store—preferably one where all the labels are not in your first language—and make a list of the most exciting snacks you can find. Bonus if they contain a flavor you've never tried before.

H'LO!

Research the best flea market or vintage shops in town and hunt for a specific item. Take pictures along the way. Write about your adventure and the treasures you saw.

How to Build a Postcard Collection

Postcards are the friendly text messages of mailed correspondence: easy to send at random, best when offered up freely and regularly, full of inside jokes and stray observations. Unlike texts, however, postcards are not private—they are not the medium you want to use if you need to deliver terrible news, or send steamy NSFW love notes, or divulge long-held family secrets. Postcards are for sending mere moments after you think about sending one.

I recommend keeping a designated postcard box near your desk (mine is a saggy, battered Birkenstocks box) and filling it with a generous and constantly regenerating supply of random postcards, along with a few sheets of stamps so you don't have to go far to find them. Special "postcard rate" stamps are cheaper, but regular stamps will work on a postcard just as well if you don't mind overpaying by a few cents. Also, if you want to send a postcard abroad from the United States, there are no global "postcard rate" stamps. It costs exactly the same to send an international postcard as it does to fling a hefty letter across an ocean. Make it make sense, USPS!

THORVALDSEN: JASON MED DET GYLDNE SKIND

HILSEN FRA DANMARK

Nearly thirty years after the advent of the postcard in Europe, Americans began buying postcards in droves. Marketers for the 1893 Columbian Exposition—the World's Fair held in Chicago— printed official fair postcards for visitors to bring home as souvenirs. The photographic cards became a routine part of the World's Fair experience and the trend caught like wildfire.

C. ST. ENERET

INCOMPLETE LIST OF POSTCARDS YOU CAN FIND ON THE INTERNET

✳ Technicolor snapshots of the Venice piazza in the 1960s

✳ Kitschy neon Florida tourism cards from the 1980s

✳ Linen postcards from the '50s, featuring California garlic fields or Colorado mountains

✳ Gibson Girl cards from the early twentieth century

✳ Bart Simpson or MacBeth or Cyndi Lauper or Nina Simone or Anna May Wong or pressed flowers or photographs of Irving Penn

✳ Museums have the best postcards: Search the online gift shops of places like Madame Tussaud's, London's Victoria and Albert Museum, the Cooper-Hewitt, the Isabella Stewart Gardiner Museum, and other institutions for their best offerings

✳ Cheesy souvenir cards from gas stations or tourist trap emporia

How to Write a Postcard

These days, the humble postcard, once all the rage in the postal world, has become something of a novelty item. Most people purchase their postcards now in museum gift shops (where they are thick, firm, and cost $3 apiece) or on spinning wire carousels while on vacation (where they tend to be kitschy, flimsy, and negotiable in price). Sure, sometimes you'll actually remember to mail a "Wish You Were Here" that serves as both a hello and a humblebrag. But most postcards end up never reaching a mailbox. Instead, they live on refrigerator doors and in desk drawers; they double as bookmarks and desk adornments. I fully understand the allure of keeping postcards for oneself—my office is full of postcards that I originally bought to send and ended up propping up against potted plants and perfume bottles or tacking onto a wall as tiny objects d'art to look at while I write. I believe wholeheartedly in buying and surrounding yourself with postcards that give your eyes a beautiful place to land when they are roaming. That said, the postcard is still a vital and often inventive correspondence medium, and I am here to tell you about the many joys of becoming a Postcard Person.

For a long time, I never really understood the allure of sending postcards through the mail other than to provide physical evidence that you really went somewhere. They seemed to serve a forensic function, incontrovertible proof that you made it to Niagara Falls or Paris or Bangkok. If you were in another country, it was a fun excuse to buy and use foreign stamps, and to have a reason to wander around hunting for a local mailbox. But you couldn't really write meaty messages there, or anything you wanted to keep private. As a tool for written communication, it felt woefully lacking.

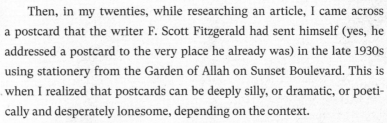

Then, in my twenties, while researching an article, I came across a postcard that the writer F. Scott Fitzgerald had sent himself (yes, he addressed a postcard to the very place he already was) in the late 1930s using stationery from the Garden of Allah on Sunset Boulevard. This is when I realized that postcards can be deeply silly, or dramatic, or poetically and desperately lonesome, depending on the context.

In 1937, F. Scott Fitzgerald took a train across the country from North Carolina, where his wife, Zelda, was staying at a mental institution, to Los Angeles, where his agent promised him enough screenwriting work that he could afford to pay Zelda's hospital bills. He was forty years old and $40,000 in debt. His novels were out of print. He had not published a book since *Tender Is the Night* in 1934, and an MGM contract was a lucrative and stable alternative. In Hollywood, he moved into an apartment complex called the Garden of Allah, a popular landing place for writers from the East Coast (famous residents included Dorothy Parker and Robert Benchley). The place had once been the glamorous grotto of a Russian silent film star named Alla Nazimova, who had built the swimming pool in the shape of the Black Sea to remind her of home. But Nazimova—and her Slavic accent, thick as black bread—could not transition to talking pictures. So she had to chop up her beloved estate and sell it for parts, converting it into bungalows where writers and artists from the East stayed when they wanted to convince themselves that they hadn't really relocated to Los Angeles. Her private utopia became a public way station for transients—even Alla, who still lived in the main house, became a specter on her own property. Tenants reported sightings of her as if they were tracking a Yeti who slunk around in oversized satin kimonos.

The Garden of Allah was the sort of purgatorial place where it was easy to dip in and out of time, the sort of place where you could pretend to exist in so many places at once that you stopped recognizing yourself in the mirror. Even though life there could feel shiny—on hot days, there were so many contract players bobbing around in the pool that it looked like starlet soup—it also could seem unreal. Barely anyone ate the food at the restaurant in the main house, which featured scratchy gray carpet that used to be pink, and served flavorless, watery bisque. What people did best at the Garden of Allah was drink, both together and alone. No one really saw the place as a permanent residence, even if they squatted there for years. It was a place to hide out in public, to disappear in plain sight.

At some point, during the nine months that Scott lived at the hotel in a second-floor bungalow, he wrote a postcard to himself. He scribbled this note in sloping, bubbly cursive on official Garden stationery and stuck a three-cent stamp on it, but he never put it in the mail. I've always wondered why he bothered to add postage. Perhaps he wanted the note to feel as if it had a distinct sender and recipient; to confirm that there were two separate selves on either end of the interaction. Perhaps he was simply bored and lonely and found himself holding a pen. Perhaps he was drunk. "Dear Scott," he wrote. Addressing himself so formally, so tenderly. "How are you? Have been meaning to come in and see you. I have [been] living at the Garden of Allah. Yours, Scott." Maybe he meant this as a joke. Maybe he did it as a way of confirming that he was still alive, still going, if not far from home and working in a medium that did not come naturally to him. Three years later, he died of a heart attack in the home of his mistress, the gossip columnist Sheilah Graham.

Fitzgerald was a dynamic and elegant letter writer—his long letters to his daughter Scottie are some of my favorites. (In one he sent when Scottie was eleven, he made a list of things to worry about, including courage and horsemanship, and things not to worry about, including boys, the future, and "insects in general.") But this postcard! It is such a sly and sad piece of ephemera and I think about it all the time. A postcard is a way of marking your place in the world; how much he must have felt like he was disintegrating if he needed to remind himself of just where his body was.

I started to see postcards as the ideal medium for sending spontaneous dispatches

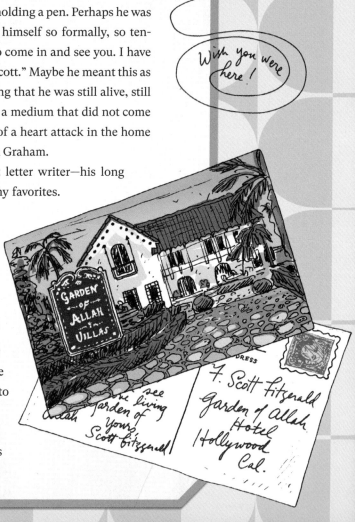

BATHERS UNDER

to anyone at any time, the moment they cross your mind. You need not take a trip to send a souvenir from wherever you are—think of postcards as snapshots from a state of mind. To me, postcards are perfect for sending generously and at random to people in your address book. They should show up as a total surprise, with the intention to delight, using only a small square of writing space. I have one pen pal, Krupa, in San Francisco, whom I have been sending postcards back and forth with for years now. On each postcard, we jot down a short list of things we loved recently and fling them across the country at each other. She will write "dill, Italian vermouth, and geoduck sashimi that tastes like tender coconut with a hint of the sea" one week and "velvet wallpaper, the parrot park, and lavender syrup" the next. I truly hope we send these brief glimpses back and forth for the rest of our lives—they feel like the perfect use of a postcard; quick and cheap to send and full of strange beauty.

Postcards are a great form for tiptoeing back in touch with someone you haven't corresponded with in a while (I always like to send a short postcard to restart a mail volley with someone I have lost touch with, as a long letter can feel a bit intimidating), but they are also an excellent in-between-letters placeholder to someone you already write to frequently. I am fast and loose with postcards when it comes to people I tend to write long letters to; I particularly like to send them to promise that a letter is coming soon. Be free with your postcards! Send them to everyone! Nobody has ever been sad to get a postcard in the mail. Best of all, they require no response. You can include a return address if you want to, but a reply is not really the point. This is what makes postcards a true luxury to receive: They ask so little of you except that you look at them. They are one-way notes passed to you from some other place, a friendly wave from the ether. You may tack them up on your fridge, or you may never think about them again. But somewhere out there, someone took the two minutes to jot down your name and toss a thin piece of cardboard your way, and that can be enough to bolster you. And if nobody is out there sending you postcards, you can always send them to yourself.

wish you were here!

HOW TO DEVELOP STYLE
IN YOUR CORRESPONDENCE

"You gotta have style," Diana Vreeland, the legendary fashion editrix, who ran both *Vogue* and *Harper's Bazaar*, once said. "It helps you get down the stairs. It helps you get up in the morning." Vreeland herself had oodles of style—by which I mean she was an absolute eccentric who formed her own opinions, often running contrary to the currents of popular tastes, about what she found interesting and alluring and exciting.

In 1955, she hired her friend, the designer Billy Baldwin, to redo the living room in her Park Avenue apartment and told him that she wanted it to look like "a garden, but a garden in hell." What he ended up doing is so wild—bright scarlet walls, giant chintz fabric curtains, red florals and paisley *everywhere*, velvet throw pillows that looked like playing cards, and lava lamps. It was like a murder scene in an Italian giallo film taking place in the Valentines' aisle of CVS, like a crate of pomegranates that exploded all over a Laura Ashley bedspread. And yet . . . it wasn't dull. "I can't imagine becoming bored with red," Vreeland allegedly once said. "It would be like becoming bored with the person you love."

Vreeland, who was born in 1903 in Paris to a wealthy family and who studied ballet and became a society debutante after moving to New York in the 1910s, was full of such bon mots; she spoke in strange, elliptical sentences and made cavalier pronouncements. When someone asked her once about her top fashion icons, she smirked and answered that she found racehorses more stylish than any person, because they always have a little "extra pizzazz" when being led into the ring. It takes a very particular, gingery brain to run *Vogue* and still say that you find actual horses far more attractive than clotheshorses; but then, Vreeland was a one of a kind. She was a geyser of sumptuous language, often deploying two-word phrases that rattle off the tongue like shiny baubles: "devastatingly chic" and "simply divine." Diana Vreeland loved adverbs almost as much as she loved jaunty cloche hats and velvet caftans, which is to say to an extreme degree. It seems that being around her might have been like being around an older, slightly deranged Eloise. Was it exhausting? Probably! But it was also enthralling. And that's *style*, baby.

Diana Vreeland wrote plenty of letters—one of my very favorite archives to pore through in the New York Public Library on Fifth Avenue is her collection of postcards, which she would send friends and fellow editors throughout her travels, often with just a single sentence on them. (She would, for example, send a note about how red was the color of the season after seeing the running of the bulls in Spain.) But, mostly, she wrote memos. Using a typewriter, she wrote them every day—to her employees, to fashion designers, to dinner party companions. She would muse on the sartorial trends of the day ("Nobody in their right mind would wear a floppy brim") or cast herself as a wisdom-dispensing oracle ("I sincerely believe that energy grows from itself and the more energy you expand the more you create within yourself"). In 2017, Rizzoli published Vreeland's memos in a hulking coffee table book; it is a dazzling conversation piece for your living room and it might be very useful when developing your own letter-writing technique.

This is not to say that you should sound like Diana Vreeland in your letters—not at all. You should not try to sound like *anyone* else—if you do, there will be a hollowness to your prose, a cool draftiness that blows through your words where warmth should be. But—and this is my most sincere tip about how to develop one's eye for anything, including a correspondence style—you must feed and nurture your curiosity. You should be reading other people's letters all the time, not to copy their prose but to get a sense of how they found their own voice within the medium. A good writer is an even better *reader*; as Vreeland famously said, "The eye has to travel," and the same goes for the pen. The first step to finding your own letter-writing élan is to read far and wide, voraciously and without hesitation. Pick up every letter collection you can (scour used bookstores, which are bursting with them) and turn to a random page; what tricks can you glean for your own correspondence, and how can you riff on them so that they become yours?

Take one of my favorite collections of correspondence, *What There Is to Say, We Have Said*, which gathers the letters between the Pulitzer Prize–winning novelist and short story writer Eudora Welty and her editor (who was also an accomplished novelist), William Maxwell. I keep the book by my desk and pull it out whenever I want to read two people writing stylishly back and forth about flowers and fruit and summer storms and literature. "Figs look hopeful this year," Welty wrote to Maxwell in 1956, ". . . just the thought of a bowl of cold ripe ones with cream on them for breakfast is worth all the rest of July . . ." In his reply, writing about pesky beetles that are eating his roses, Maxwell wrote, "[W]hen I come on the shreds of one that was exquisite in the morning and raddled by noon, I have murder in my heart." Cold ripe figs! Raddled roses! There is a brisk elegance to their letters that is like salt air.

Sometimes, however, I am looking more for a disheveled, punk style than refined sophistication (when I want more Vivienne Westwood than Charles James), and I'll turn to *I'm Very into You*, a collection of email correspondence from the nineties (when email was, essentially, a dynamic epistolary form and not the overcrowded, junk-filled Gmail inboxes we avoid today) between the writers McKenzie Wark and the late novelist and poet Kathy Acker. Acker often wrote unsparing missives to her friends. Here she is telling Wark that her swelling notoriety as an author is not enough to pay the bills:

←FIRST FOLD HERE→

TO OPEN CUT HERE →

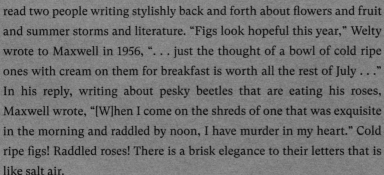

a filmy stole clipped to top of bodice

Only a few years later, Acker died of cancer—her anger was justified, palpable. And yet it was still full of a style and rhythm only she could conjure; the capital letters, the parentheses, the use of ellipses. Style, in letter writing, can be the way you use punctuation, or the way you don't. (A fun exercise: Write an entire letter that is one long, breathless sentence.) Your letters can be whatever you want them to be: glittering or funny or rageful or confusing or mysterious or forceful or straightforward or withholding or saccharine or deadly serious—what matters is that you are playing around, trying to find your way to something that only you can produce.

Style is something you stumble your way into; it's a state of exploration rather than a state of arrival. You do not need a lot of frippery to have style—just as Vreeland said that her definition of the word has very little to do with having lots of clothes—and you don't need a fancy fountain pen or expensive stationery or a feather quill to write iconic letters. You just need to follow your instincts. Are you moved to create an oddball signature sign-off? Do you feel like writing only on found materials, like the backs of bills or cereal boxes? Do you want to include a hand-drawn illustration or write in the form of a graphic novel? Do you want to include a collage

with every letter? Do you want to secretly pick five random vocabulary words and always work them into a letter, no matter what? Do you want to write as a character? Where your instincts and your creativity intersect, you will begin to forge your own way.

There are benefits to developing a unique letter-writing aesthetic—people will be all the more excited to rip open your letters, anticipating what is waiting for them inside. You will also be creating a body of work, rather than simply sending off pieces of paper—one that will be a delight to read years later (and, in a small bid for immortality, one that might even be worth publishing). You will know, when you sit down to write, not only how to begin but how to keep surprising yourself; style is, at best, a foundation that you can constantly keep building on, subverting, and shifting. It can evolve, just as you do. But it is an anchor, a place to start and a place to end. Write the kind of letters that would make Diana Vreeland proud—add a little extra *pizzazz*. Maintaining a regular correspondence, in a world where letters are both antiquated and cumbersome, is already as stylish as it gets; now all you have to do to really take it over the top is add a few of your own accessories.

"Oh, my Dear Friend, my heart was trembling as I walked into the post office, and there you were, lying in Box 237. I took you out of your envelope and read you, read you right there."

—actress Margaret Sullavan, as the letter-loving shopgirl Klara Novak in the 1940 film *The Shop Around the Corner*

84 Charing Cross Road (1987): Anne Bancroft plays a writer in Manhattan who falls for an antiquarian bookseller in London, played by Anthony Hopkins. They spend years writing to each other about literature! Steamy!

The Shop Around the Corner (1940): A salesgirl at a department store absolutely *loathes* her coworker, but she loves the mystery man she has been writing letters to . . . and, of course, as it turns out, they are the same person.

You've Got Mail (1998): An update of *Shop Around the Corner,* infused with Nora Ephron's trademark wit and bounce. It has everything: Meg Ryan, Tom Hanks, and Greg Kinnear delivering an impassioned monologue about typewriters; Parker Posey drinking too much espresso; and a very handsome dog named Brinkley.

Mary and Max (2009): An Australian stop-motion animation fantasia about the unlikely pen pal friendship between an eight-year-old Australian girl (Toni Collette) and an elderly man in Manhattan (Phillip Seymour Hoffman).

Legends of the Fall (1994): Brad Pitt! Tortured love notes! Cowboy hats!

Sleepless in Seattle (1993): Another delightful Nora Ephron film that hangs on correspondence. After hearing Sam (Tom Hanks) on the radio, Annie (Meg Ryan) writes him a fan letter so wonderful that Sam's son runs away to New York to find her.

Can You Ever Forgive Me? (2018): Melissa McCarthy plays the real-life forgery artist Lee Israel, who created and sold hundreds of fake letters by famous writers in the nineties. Equal parts poignant, cozy, and devastating.

Letters to Juliet (2010): A winning romance about a magazine fact-checker (Amanda Seyfried), who travels to Italy and finds out that many women who visit the town of Verona write letters to the fictional Shakespeare heroine Juliet Capulet, asking them for love advice. When she finds an old "letter to Juliet" from the 1950s (written by a woman played by Vanessa Redgrave) and decides to answer it herself, she kicks off a madcap series of events.

PUTTING TOGETHER A LETTERS-THEMED FILM FESTIVAL

Before cell phones made it possible to contact anyone, anywhere, at any time, and people had to communicate through writing, there were a whole lot more missed connections and mix-ups, thwarted correspondences and unanswered pleas. There was no guarantee that a love letter, once scribbled, would not fall into the wrong hands. Signals got crossed, people grew apart, yearning swelled to epic proportions. The dramatic opportunities presented by letter-writing were delicious and undeniable. Give me a mysterious letter that arrives on a doorstep, and I'm hooked! A person who ghosts another via text message simply doesn't hit the same as a passionate epistolary romance that devolves into chaos. People say the cell phone killed the rom com, and while I don't think that's entirely true, it almost certainly killed the screwball comedy, a genre that relies on the farcical hijinks that can come along with not having all the information available to you at your fingertips. Still, thanks to the magic of modern technology, you can now stream all of the marvelous movies made about letters in the past. There is, of course, Ernest Lubitsch's sparkling 1940 film *The Shop Around the Corner,* in which a shop girl in New York City begins writing swoony letters with a secret admirer, only to find out that she has been writing with her work nemesis all along. In 1998, Nora Ephron, a lifelong believer in the theatrical potential of the postal service, remade *The Shop Around the Corner* as *You've Got Mail,* which swaps out handwritten communiqués for emails (letters also feature prominently in Ephron's 1993 film, *Sleepless in Seattle*).

At left, you'll find a brief list—in no particular order—of films that hinge upon letter writing, in all its cinematic splendor. Break out the popcorn.

A Brief Taxonomy of Envelopes

You simply cannot send a letter without an envelope (unless you send a postcard, but *is* a postcard a letter? Discuss)—and yet! Envelopes have somehow gotten a reputation as the most boring, banal, basic aspect of correspondence—the thing you stick other things into. The blah exterior you must tear open and cast aside to reveal the treasures within. But when you really think about it, envelopes can be downright sensual. First, the word: Its use as a paper good dates back to France in the 1700s, but it comes from the Middle English word *envolupen*, which meant "to be involved in" some kind of naughty business (crime, adultery, other sinful and hedonistic acts). The modern equivalent, *envelop*, is not necessarily so dirty but the word isn't exactly clean, either. Think about telling someone you want to "envelop them" and things get intimate pretty quickly. It's a steamy word!

So why have envelopes become such a quotidian part of sending mail? I blame everything on the #10 "business envelope," the classic 4⅛-inch by 9½-inch varieties that tend to contain something you don't want: bills, insurance claim denials, magazine subscription notices, credit card spam, jury summonses, college rejection letters. Because we send so few letters for pleasure these days, envelopes have become more threatening than thrilling. When was the last time you opened up an envelope with your hand *trembling* with excitement? If you have to think, it has been too long. But to get envelopes that set your heart aflutter—and that give you an excuse to buy a good letter opener—you have to give them. Beautiful envelopes beget beautiful envelopes. Think of envelopes as the pajamas of the letter-writing world: You don't need them to be elegant, and any old ratty T-shirt will do in a pinch. But life is a lot more fun if you sleep in silk.

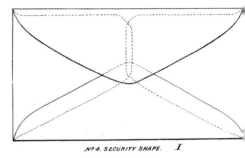

Nº 4. SECURITY SHAPE. *I*

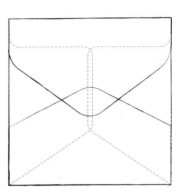

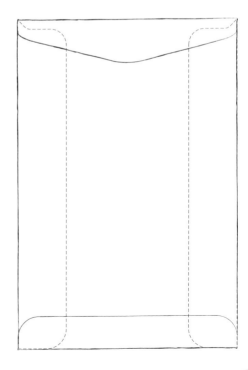

BUSINESS IN THE FRONT, PARTY ON THE FLAP

It is a shame that long, lean envelopes have become the main signifiers of junk mail, because they are a nearly perfect mail vessel: sleek, refined, mail-slot compliant, the perfect size for trifolding paper. It is time to reclaim the "business" envelope from its milquetoast origins and start using it during off-hours. Think of them as the dachshunds of the envelope kingdom—stretched and elegant while still playful.

CREAMY DREAMY

Is there anything more satisfying than getting a substantial eggshell-textured envelope in the mail? Luxurious envelopes usually contain momentous news: wedding details, baby or graduation announcements, gala invitations, an extra tiny envelope that requires you to select chicken or fish. But what if you sent them *just because*?

VELLUM

Vellum envelopes come in all shapes and colors but share one quality—they are slightly see-through, like a mesh top, or a gauzy window curtain. They leave little to the imagination, and yet they don't reveal everything. One fun way to use them is to put a colorful postcard or photograph inside that peeks through ever so subtly and whispers, "Open me." Vellum envelopes are practically burlesque.

KRAFT PAPER

Kraft paper envelopes are an inviting blank canvas for mail art. Against the rustic brown tint, any extra embellishments—stickers, stamps, hot-glued lace or ribbon, wax seals, ripped-up bits of sheet music or dime-store novels or magazines—stand out in bold relief. Search Instagram for the #mailart hashtag and you will see hundreds of butcher-paper envelopes pop up, all covered in scribbles and magpie-esque collage. So go make some mail art!

TECHNICOLOR

My very favorite envelope store—yes, there are envelope stores!—on the Internet is JAM Paper, whose tagline is EVERY COLOR, EVERY SIZE. They are not kidding about the colors. They sell envelopes in sunflower yellow and antique gold, ultra-lime and racing green, "presidential blue" and lapis lazuli. I recommend logging on during a lazy Sunday and ordering a few colors that make you happy.

PEARLESCENT/HOLOGRAPHIC/METALLIC

Well, aren't *you* fancy? These are flashy envelopes for flashy people. They can feel a little gimmicky and even desperate but they can also feel defiantly festive if you send them on an average Tuesday. When it comes to shiny envelopes, the tackier the better. It should be preposterous. I recommend hot pink metallic envelopes that look like something Barbie might wear to a rave. Why not?

SECURITY

When I was a child, my parents kept a box of a hundred security envelopes in the cluttered kitchen nook where they also kept the bills. I assume they used them to keep checks and other financial documents away from prying eyes, but I would regularly swipe them for my own personal business (passing notes in class—what else?). There was (and still is!) something so evocative to me about a container meant for top-secret materials. Even if you have nothing to hide, it can be fun to pretend that you do.

WINDOW

Window envelopes are almost extinct when it comes to personal use. Can you remember the last time you got a letter in a window envelope that was not a tax bill or a nonprofit organization asking for a donation? But what if you . . . changed the view? On the off chance you find yourself in possession of a spare window envelope, it can be a joy to line up your recipient's address perfectly so that it fits inside the plastic. Get creative with it! Put in see-through colored tissue paper and make the envelope look like stained glass! With enough imagination, even envelopes can look like department store windows at Christmastime.

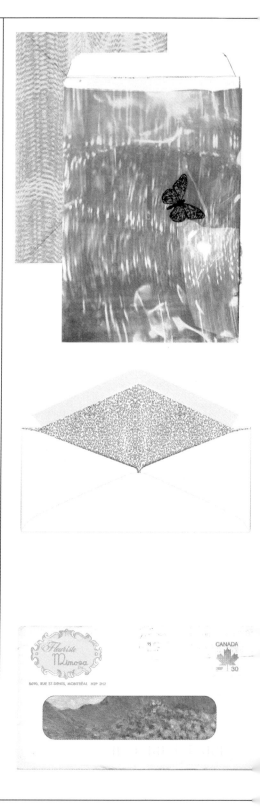

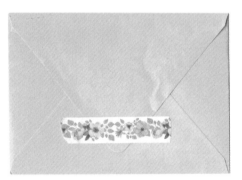

MANILA

Chances are you are not sending a manila envelope regularly through the mail, though if you find yourself needing to mail a friend a slim book or a copy of a magazine, there is no better vessel. The manila envelope has come to stand for mind-numbing corporate communication and interoffice memos, but it has quite a rich, wild history: Beginning in the 1830s, sailors who visited the Philippines began to export manila hemp, or abacá, an impressively strong fiber that comes from a native tree that bears inedible, banana-like fruit. Manila hemp was first used to make rope for ships, but soon thereafter it became a valuable material for making durable paper goods that were water-resistant and could withstand long, seafaring journeys. After the Philippine-American War of 1899, however, an already pricey export became more or less impossible to get, and manufacturers started to make cheaper envelopes out of wood pulp. Today's manila envelopes are pale imitations of the original, in that they will disintegrate when soggy and grow floppy and brittle over time. But they still have a timeless feel, and transmit a certain kind of retro, three-martini-lunch vibe.

BARONIAL

Baronial envelopes are basically regular schmegular envelopes . . . but wearing a V-neck. What makes an envelope "baronial" is the depth and shape of its top flap—it should be pointed and hit at the center of the envelope or below. You encounter these envelopes all the time, as they are the bread and butter of the greeting card industry. But now you know they have a stuffy and superfluous name!

SQUARE

Square envelopes: fun to send, fun to receive, a nightmare for the USPS's standard sorting machines. If you do go square, be sure to add extra postage. Every year, the postal service comes out with a "non-machinable surcharge" stamp just for using on square envelopes. The cost basically says, "Your voluptuous and impractical envelope messes with our entire automated system and we therefore have to process it by hand. Kindly pay us extra for ruining our day."

Pink Paper

(OR FINDING YOUR INNER JACQUELINE SUSANN)

One day, while sitting at my desk and struck with a sudden case of the low-stakes shoppies (a brief and mostly harmless condition that causes you to feel that you absolutely *must* purchase something small in an attempt to replenish your serotonin), I ordered a six-pack of pink legal-ruled notepads.

I was brand-agnostic at first. Having since sampled several varietals of pink lined paper, I can report that they are not all created equal. I'm currently loyal to the Roaring Spring "Enviroshades" pad, which comes in the creamy, chalky pink of a Necco conversation heart and has lines that are wide enough to accommodate loopy script but thin enough that you feel adult, and not like a second grader practicing cursive. If you are feeling slightly more adventurous, you might try the Tops "Prism Plus" lined pad, a generous ream that comes in the nauseating and yet compelling shade of barely cooked salmon (or is it kitten tongue?). For the nonconformists, there are also endless options for blush-colored paper without lines at all—Office Depot copy paper (a milky flamingo color, like radioactive Pepto-Bismol), Boise "Fireworx" paper (a pink as light and delicate as a rose macaron), and Astrobright sheets in "plasma pink," a neon hue that calls to mind the 1920s fashion designer Elsa Schiaparelli's infamous "shocking pink," a blaring magenta that she described as "bright, impossible, impudent, becoming, life-giving, like all the lights and the birds and the fish in the world put together." It had never before occurred to me that paper could be impudent, but that was before I started thinking pink.

My first order of bubblegum paper was spontaneous, but the underlying desire was premeditated. I was possessed by the idea of writing on pink pads for several weeks before I pulled the trigger, and it was all

HOW TO FIND PAPER THAT IS VERY YOU

Stationery is as personal as undergarments or bed linens—which is to say, I simply cannot choose what is best for you. I can, of course, tell you about beautiful hand-marbled paper from Italy, or adorable Japanese stationery with see-through cellophane boxes that make your envelopes look like the windows of a cat café. I can tell you about the boxed writing paper sets from the Pepin Press (an American printing house that grew out of the legendary Dutch graphic designer Pepin Van Roojen's one-man stationery company in the 1980s) that feature antique city maps or swirling Art Nouveau patterns. I can tell you about the thousands of sellers on Etsy who make one-of-a-kind notecards and stationery sets, featuring everything from barn owls to Bruce Springsteen to rare types of mushrooms. I can direct you to sites where you can buy neon printer paper, or yellow legal pads, or recycled paper in bulk. I can point you toward cheap airmail envelopes and pricey British stationery that costs more than a bottle of good Champagne.

But the truth is that one of the purest joys of letter-writing is in finding your own way to the paper that feels like you. There will be a lot of trial and error. I spent more money than I would like to admit building up a collection of pastel floral stationery that I thought would be very granny-chic but ultimately made me feel depressed every time I pulled it out. I found that my style is colorful and quirky and that it is in constant flux. I am always on the hunt, always keeping my eyes open. Just the other day, I ordered a box of vintage Muppet-themed "postalettes"—a Hallmark product from the 1980s and 1990s that was a single sheet of thick paper that folds up into its own envelope—and perhaps that will be my new calling card. Until the next thing.

WHERE HAVE YOU BEEN OWL NIGHT.

Jacqueline Susann's fault. Let me explain: During the long winter lock-down of 2020, I spent several hours soaking in the crumbling porcelain bathtub in my walk-up apartment and rereading Susann's frothy, trashy, glamorous, gossipy, bitchy, striving, harrowing, soapy 1966 novel *Valley of the Dolls*. It felt like the perfect book to sink into when there was nowhere much to go; it is, after all, a story about how treacherous it can be to strive for more than just a hot bath and a hot meal.

The book tells the story of three striving women in Manhattan: Anne Welles, an industrious secretary at a theatrical agency; Jennifer North, a flailing and boy-crazy actress whose beauty far outpaces her talent; and Neely O'Hara, a singer with the chops to become a real star and the nar-cissistic tendencies to become a real nightmare. All three women attempt to climb whatever ladders are available to them in 1960s New York City: nightclub gigs, advantageous marriages, lucrative modeling contracts, titillating roles in French "art films," affairs of the heart, affairs of conve-nience, Broadway marquees. They also succumb to drug addiction, alco-holism, depression, and despair. Jennifer gets breast cancer and swallows a fistful of "dolls"—Susann's nickname for various prescription pills—when she learns that her cancer is terminal (Susann herself received a breast cancer diagnosis before *Valley of the Dolls* was pub-lished and had a radical double mastectomy in 1962, a fact she concealed from her publishers and even her closest friends). Neely has a drunken meltdown and lands in a sanitarium. Anne has a baby with a man who will never stop cheating on her. The entire thing would be a brutal bummer if it wasn't so deliriously fun.

According to her editor, Michael Korda, Jac-queline Susann wrote her first drafts on pink paper. She plunked out sentences in all caps on her pink IBM electric typewriter, and then, Korda wrote in the *New Yorker*, she "added revisions in a large, forceful circular hand, with what looked like a

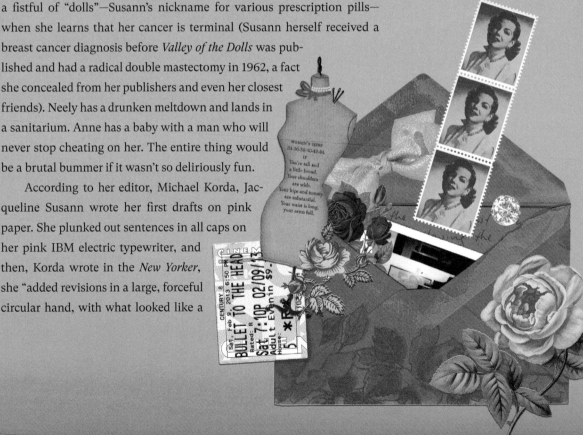

blunt eyebrow pencil." However, there is some dispute as to what draft Susann chose to commit to pink; her husband, Irving Mansfield, wrote in his memoir *Life with Jackie* that she had a complex color-coded system that involved a rainbow of reams: "The rough run through was on cheap white sheets. The next rewrite was on yellow, and in that draft, Jackie concentrated on her characters. The third version was on pink, and it stressed story and motivation."

Susann worked on the book for a year and a half inside her apartment at the Navarro, a residential hotel on Fifty-Ninth Street and Sixth Avenue near the entrance to Central Park (one perk of living in a hotel was that she could have tuna fish sandwiches—her favorite food—brought up to her at all hours of the day; perhaps the secret to a prolific writing career is good room service). She wore pigtails as she wrote, a strange, girlish impulse for working on a book about such adult behavior as adultery and drug binges, but, then, Susann was a woman who valued strange ritual above all things. She wrote from ten to five every day, with her telephone unplugged. (This was a real sacrifice: When she wasn't writing, Susann was endlessly gossiping in order to have material to write about.) Then she retired for a cocktail with Irving every night around six. After dinner, she made calls. In a way, Susann was corresponding with people all the time, only she did it with a pink rotary phone while wearing a peignoir nightgown.

Valley of the Dolls was a smash hit even before it became a feature film. "Jackie, it seemed, understood by instinct that her readers were ready for the raw side of love—for crude behavior, abortions, suicide," Korda wrote. "Perhaps more important, she and Irving created a new way of selling a novel—a shameless blend of promotion, personal appearances, and celebrity tie-ins." Susann was a tireless workhorse when it came to pushing her own product; she haunted the late-night circuit and showed up at her publisher's warehouse to shake the hands of the deliverymen who shuttled copies of the book to stores. All the while, Susann was harboring a secret. In 1962, before she ever started writing *Valley* (or even her first book, *Every Night Josephine!*—a successful, silly memoir about living with her beloved Standard Poodle), Susann learned that she had terminal breast cancer. She had a full mastectomy the day after Christmas of 1962. Right before the surgery, she wrote in her diary, "I can't die without leaving something—something big. . . . I'm Jackie—I have a dream. I think I can write. Let me live to make it!"

The book is, undoubtedly, a soapy, schlocky mess that can feel as sticky and indulgent as melted taffy, but that's what makes it so compulsive to read. Susann knew how to *sell*, and how to sell herself. Irving, who started working full time as her manager, finagled over 250 television appearances for her to hock her literary wares, and the book stayed on the *New York Times* bestseller list for sixty-five consecutive weeks. "Jackie knew how to manipulate every conversation right back to the book," her publisher Bernard Geis told *Vanity Fair* reporter Amy Fine Collins. "It got to the point where you could not turn on a water faucet without getting Jacqueline Susann."

Susann died in 1974, at only fifty-six, having written several bestsellers. She wanted to become a household name, and she manifested it through sheer will. But, also, through pink paper. She sweated over her manuscript, even when the sentences were clumsy, even when she had no idea how it would all turn out. She had faith in those pink pages. She oozed self-belief onto the page in loopy eye pencil. I will never not think of her when I pick up a piece of pink paper and drag it through my typewriter to begin a letter: all of that striving, all of that desperation, all of that urgent desire to live long enough to see yourself make waves.

I love writing letters on pink paper, and I would encourage you to try it. Letters are, for better or worse, always a first draft. Unless you are a very special kind of obsessive, you probably don't sit down to edit your letters or make longhand revisions. You just type, or scribble, and send. Everything you write in a letter has the swagger of fresh confidence, the crispness of the maiden pass. It's coming hot off the presses, every time. You don't have to write on pink paper, but perhaps you can find *your* version of it: What is the paper that gets

Syme's Letter Writer

you excited to sit down and spool out words where they did not exist before? What paper will become your signature, the calling card that will outlive you? What paper induces a ritual, a space of play and creativity, a space where the future could be bright if only you can live to see it, where you can do and be something *big*?

Try switching to colored paper for your next few letters. Pour all of your gossip, your sweeping theories, your hopes and frustrations and petty concerns onto those pages. And then, seal them up and pour yourself a martini.

The Best Cures for the Epistolary Shoppies

Sometimes, seemingly out of nowhere, I am beset by a modern condition that I have come to call the aforementioned "shoppies," or that feeling when you absolutely must purchase something, any little thing—as a treat, as a distraction or procrastination, or even as a self-administered reward for some minor and barely admirable achievement like clearing out your inbox or remembering to pay the electric bill on time. The shoppies can strike at any moment, but they tend to follow predictable patterns: They show up on rainy days, or recently after heartbreak, or whenever a paycheck hits your account and for a few moments you are feeling flush before calculating more practical expenses. They show up after a few cocktails, or on a lazy weekend afternoon, or during the workday when you have an important deadline looming and yet find yourself browsing deeply discounted vintage strappy sandals online (and you don't even wear strappy sandals).

I try to advise friends who are in the grip of the shoppies not to go within two blocks of a Sephora or a local bookstore; the shoppies are the reason that you have a drawer full of random lip glosses in the same color and a stack of unused blank notebooks even though you have not fully filled up a notebook in years. The shoppies can be equally dangerous and productive, profligate and giddy. The key to riding the wave when the shoppies hit is to focus your desire on small, affordable items, and all in one category (it is the wild flailing between clothes and artisanal foodstuffs and fresh flowers and decorative knickknacks that will get you in trouble). Fortunately, I have found the world of correspondence to be a perfect outlet for the shoppies. You will almost never regret building out your letter-writing drawer (or, in my case . . . cabinet) in order to give yourself more options for when you finally sit down to write.

Book of Kells

Here, I offer a list of ways and places to stock your correspondence coffers. The hunt is half the thrill, so I always recommend in-person browsing, but shopping online for inks and paper can be surprisingly delightful these days. Individual stores come and go, but I encourage you to shop at independent retailers when you can. Support your corner stationery store!

STATIONERY STORES: I simply cannot recommend seeking out paper-goods stores enough—both in your own area and when you are traveling. New York City is big enough to have several such stores with different themes— one that just sells colorful Japanese stationery, another devoted to marbled Italian paper, another that sells very formal engraved cards to Upper East Side doyennes, another that sells only graphite pencils. Tokyo, Paris, Florence, and London are all legendary for their stationery stores, but you can find amazing paper purveyors in out-of-the-way places. You just have to look. **Good for: Stationery (naturally), fountain pens, wax-seal supplies, washi tape, paper ephemera**

MUSEUM SHOPS: The secret MVP for anyone who writes letters, museum gift shops are treasure troves of sturdy pens, artful paper, and other eccentric ephemera suitable for mailing. I love going to a museum gift shop and putting together a thick envelope full of little trinkets I find there—flat filigree ornaments, glossy fridge magnets, gilded tarot cards, joke-y socks. I no longer allow myself to go into museum stores when I have the shoppies because I want everything, but I encourage you to test your own limits. **Good for: Postcards, artful boxed notecard sets, bookmarks, sticky notes, oddball souvenirs**

ONLINE PEN AND INK STORES: In the last decade, the pen Internet has really come into its own (see page 130). There is now a glut of wonderful pen suppliers with delightful web presences, some of whom have vibrant YouTube channels where they review pens, demonstrate inflow, and showcase various nibs—a soothing place to disappear into for a while. JetPens is the granddaddy of the bunch (and still the best place to buy gel pens and rollerballs), but newer sellers like Goulet Pens, Goldspot, Pen Chalet,

How to Develop Style in Your Correspondence

Atlas Stationers, and others are always open for your insomniac scrolling needs. If you need calligraphy supplies, John Neal Books, which has been selling nibs and inkwells since 1981, is a classic choice, or you can look to modern calligraphy experts like the Postman's Knock and Calligrafile. If you are looking for one-of-a-kind fountain pen ink, try the Birmingham Ink Company, Noodler's Ink, Diamine Inks, J. Herbin, or Ferris Wheel Press. **Good for: Fountain pens (from entry-level to very fancy), gel pens in bulk, glitter markers, hard-to-find Japanese ballpoints, pen travel cases, calligraphy nibs and nib holders, ink and inkwells, feather quills**

EBAY AND ETSY: If you want to get deep into correspondence, learn to love the online peer-to-peer marketplace. eBay is still the best place to find old postcards in bulk, vintage stamps, discontinued stationery sets, and eclectic bundles of random paper (hot tip: search for "scrapbooking ephemera"). Etsy can be a bit pricier when it comes to vintage, but it is a bonanza when it comes to finding original illustrated notecards, hand-drawn stickers, or artfully curated stamp sets. **Good for: Vintage postcards, stationery and stamps, washi tape samplers, one-of-a-kind stickers and illustrated cards, odd bundles of paper ephemera, old sheet music or magazines that you can turn into envelopes**

FLEA MARKETS: I never manage to leave a flea market without finding postcards or other random items I might want to tuck into letters (black and white photographs, ticket stubs, bits of ribbon, plastic hotel key fobs). Plus, you can really find a deal—I'm still working through a shoebox of hundreds of old-school matchbooks that someone sold me for three dollars. **Good for: Affordable bric-a-brac that you can use as embellishments**

SPRING SEASON IN ISLAMABAD

Unconventional Materials

Paper is great, paper is wonderful. But sometimes, inspiration strikes (or you simply don't have any stationery nearby). I say follow your impulses to write on other surfaces. Cocktail napkins? Great. Cereal box insides you cut into shapes? Perfection. An entire letter written inside a series of matchbooks? Iconic. The back of a voided paycheck? Why not? Write a letter on the inside of a paperback novel you buy for $1 at a used bookstore and send the book along. Two gifts in one! Write freely and often, everywhere you can. Think of yourself as Harold with the purple crayon—if you can scribble on it, it should be scribbled upon. If you can mail it, it should be mailed.

From Fynes Mory:
diary of an En

93. Zounds:
96. Even no
ping:
rting
istemp
pon:
art m

EL CAMINO RESTAURANTE
CARRER DE CAN BRONDO 4, BAJO
07001 PALMA DE MALLORCA
ILLES BALEARS

www.elcaminopalma.es
correo info@el-camino.es / mesaprivada@el-camino.es
instagram el_camino_palma facebook El Camino Palma

ORBIDDEN CITY
SUTTER ST. SAN FRANCISCO

THE QUEEN OF

SAYS TO THE KING OF

HAVE A BIG

I DON'T WANT YOUR

Just take me to

CAFÉ SA

OR

XTRA

OT

FRANCAISE

CLOSE COVER BEFORE

Personalization: Chic or Not?

Monogramming has, over the years, gotten something of a dusty, aristocratic reputation. It is peak WASP culture. It is a vodka stinger before lunch with a side of repressed emotions and a tortoiseshell cigarette holder burnishing an Ultra-Light Virginia Slim. It is canvas beach bags with navy grosgrain piping. It is shell-pink ballet flats. It is billowing terry-cloth robes and striped cabana towels. It is tomato juice and tennis whites and the smell of a soft summer lawn that nobody is allowed to walk on. It is expensive flip-flops and inexpensive straw hats; it is crisp Egyptian cotton sheets with a thread count in the thousands. It is paying attention to thread count. It is leather-bound books that serve mostly as decoration. It is having a family crest and knowing what all of the symbols mean. It is going out for the lacrosse team. It is having a distant great-aunt who was institutionalized for having a "touch of hysteria" in the early twentieth century. It is discovering that great-aunt's fur coats in an attic and finding that she delicately had her initials sewn into the sateen lining of each one, right near her hip bone. It is ordering custom notecards every season from Crane or Smythson of Bond Street, with yellow-gold embossing.

But personalizing your paper need not be so stuffy an affair! I am of the opinion that glamour is what you make of it (my official definition is that glamour is what happens when your particular, passionate taste intersects with the world with full force and no apologies), and I think that personalized stationery can, in fact, be extremely glamorous. Toss out the traditional—creamy, embossed stationery is for princesses and diplomats. Go for kitschy letterhead instead—you can look at the great archive

at letterheady.com for inspiration. Make it bold. Go with Pepto pink paper with hot-pink monogramming, or butterscotch paper with forest-green accents. Have your most talented friend doodle a custom logo and put it on everything (compensate them for their work, of course, or at least offer to buy them a fancy meal). Scribble out your signature and have it printed on all of your writing materials. Go to sites like Papier or Minted, pick out your favorite design, and have them put FROM THE DESK OF _____ at the top of a fresh set of notecards. Go to Zazzle or Etsy and have custom postcards made. Order rubber stamps with your return address on them, or a wax seal bearing your monogram.

There are countless ways to customize now—the only limit is your imagination. Having your very own letterhead is incredibly chic; it is also timeless. Years after you are gone, your personalized stationery will still be floating around, whispering, *She was here, and she knew it.*

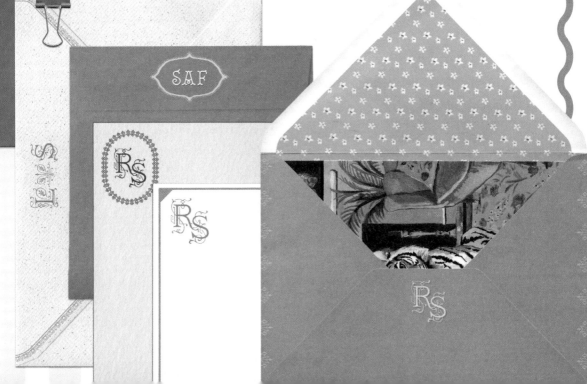

HOW TO WRITE
ABOUT CLOTHES

Everyone, everywhere gets dressed in the morning. What we choose to wear—one of the first, most definitional choices we make in the morning—is inextricably tied to who we are and who we long to be, even though many continue to dismiss fashion as frivolous and swishy and separate from serious cultural pursuits. Clothing *is* culture, however, and moreover, it is inescapable. You can choose to ignore what's on television or stop reading books, but unless you join a nudist colony, your life is going to directly intersect with fashion every time you leave the house.

The great fashion critic Kennedy Fraser, who covered the subject for the *New Yorker* in the 1970s and 1980s, described her world as one of "hints and tricks and dreams and metaphors—a place of confusing, sometimes falsified signposts where time, by running sideways or in big backward loops, contrived to stay just ahead of us all." There is nothing frivolous about paying attention to the sideways loops that both inspire us and outrun us, to the objects we put on our bodies that can change the way we move through the world on any given day. Clothing can reveal as much as it can conceal. The historian Anne Hollander, who wrote the classic book *Seeing through Clothes* (a must to keep on your bookshelf if you want to understand how trends have evolved over the eras), stated that "clothes can suggest, persuade, connote, insinuate, or indeed lie, and apply subtle pressure while their wearer is speaking frankly and straightforwardly of other matters." Fashion speaks for us, even when we have nothing else to say. Which is why I suggest that if you are stumped for something to write about in a letter, you begin with what you are wearing.

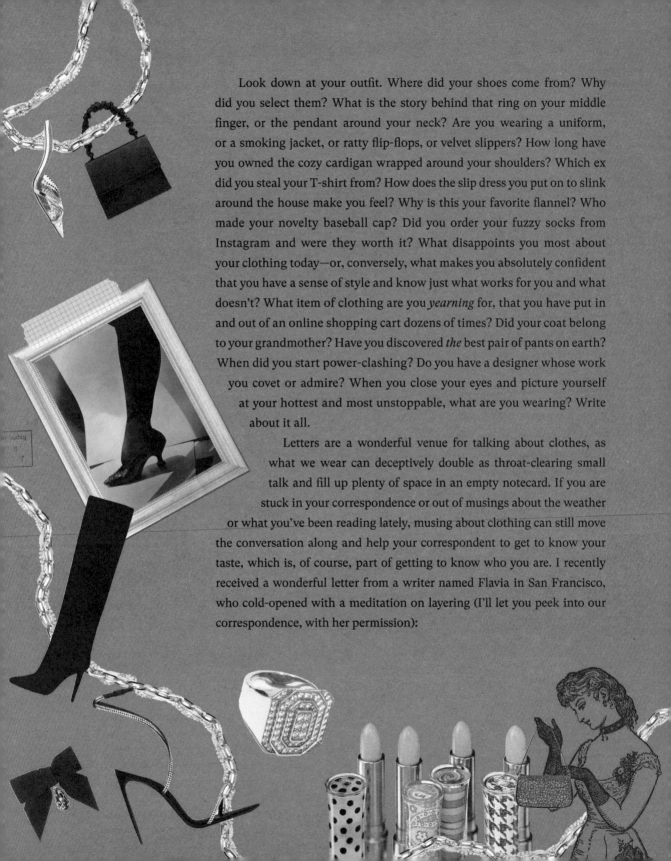

Look down at your outfit. Where did your shoes come from? Why did you select them? What is the story behind that ring on your middle finger, or the pendant around your neck? Are you wearing a uniform, or a smoking jacket, or ratty flip-flops, or velvet slippers? How long have you owned the cozy cardigan wrapped around your shoulders? Which ex did you steal your T-shirt from? How does the slip dress you put on to slink around the house make you feel? Why is this your favorite flannel? Who made your novelty baseball cap? Did you order your fuzzy socks from Instagram and were they worth it? What disappoints you most about your clothing today—or, conversely, what makes you absolutely confident that you have a sense of style and know just what works for you and what doesn't? What item of clothing are you *yearning* for, that you have put in and out of an online shopping cart dozens of times? Did your coat belong to your grandmother? Have you discovered *the* best pair of pants on earth? When did you start power-clashing? Do you have a designer whose work you covet or admire? When you close your eyes and picture yourself at your hottest and most unstoppable, what are you wearing? Write about it all.

Letters are a wonderful venue for talking about clothes, as what we wear can deceptively double as throat-clearing small talk and fill up plenty of space in an empty notecard. If you are stuck in your correspondence or out of musings about the weather or what you've been reading lately, musing about clothing can still move the conversation along and help your correspondent to get to know your taste, which is, of course, part of getting to know who you are. I recently received a wonderful letter from a writer named Flavia in San Francisco, who cold-opened with a meditation on layering (I'll let you peek into our correspondence, with her permission):

Dear Rachel,

One thing I've been wondering about recently is overcoats. In layered coats. The act of wearing several coats
at once. Every now and then, a character in a movie will
show up at a restaurant and they have a gorgeous overcoat
on, and under that a trench coat, and under that they
have a blazer, and under the blazer they have a beautiful
cashmere sweater, and under that they have an undershirt.

Now, I won't discuss the merits of the undershirt
and wool sweater—I'm not here to do that. I live in
California—Northern California, more precisely—so I'm no
stranger to the cult of layers. But it's all those coats
that have been driving me insane: where have they gone? I
seem to have failed to mention that those characters in all
those films are characters from period films. *Casablanca*
and the like. Those Audrey Hepburn films—which, yes,
span decades, but I think you get my point. I was asking
myself the other day if the world has become too warm for
all of those coats to be worn at once, or if people were
skinnier back then. I just don't see anyone dressed that
way anymore, not even in the movies. So that has been on
my mind.

"One thing I've been wondering about lately is overcoats" . . .
is there a more charming way to begin a letter? Through this
note, I got to know what Flavia thinks about when she
glances around at strangers, what her mental vocabulary
includes—Humphrey Bogart, the feeling of a lost era, an
elegiac sense that people no longer put in a wacky amount
of effort when it comes to outerwear, the "cult of layers," a
jumble of classic movies and modern curiosity. I learned
more about Flavia from this short overcoat meditation than I
had from other letters that went on for five pages.

In November 1940, Virginia Woolf, who always paid acute attention to clothing in both her fiction and her personal writing, wrote a letter to her friend, the composer and suffragist Ethel Smyth, about wearing her husband's trousers. It was the year before her death and Woolf was living at a cottage called Monk's House in Sussex, far from the roaring London that she loved—her husband Leonard believed that the countryside might offer her some respite from her growing depression and anxiety (also, a bit of distance from the blitz of bombs that were hitting the city, including one that landed near the Woolfs' London home and sent all of their books crashing to the ground. She wrote to Smith that Sussex was not entirely safe from the barrage. She wrote that the river had been bombed, and the seagulls on its banks flocked to the surface to ride the waves. Woolf went exploring out on the marsh, she writes, tripped and fell into a six-foot hole, and returned home "looking like a spaniel." She added that fortunately, she was wearing a pair of Leonard's shabby old pants. "Tomorrow," she wrote, "I buy a pair of cords for myself." In her simple shopping declaration, Woolf shows that she is actively willing herself to embrace country life, inasmuch as she can (it also speaks to her attraction to androgyny, or to subverting the fashionable norms of the day, and to women's fashion becoming freer and more liberated in general). Whatever you long to buy—be it a dress you saw in a shop window or a pair of high-top basketball shoes—does reveal something secret and hidden within your heart. Pour your material longings into a letter and see what tumbles out (also, I often find that writing about a thing—and exploring the roots of my desire for it—is often enough to put me off buying it).

HOW TO MAINTAIN A GLAMOROUS MYSTIQUE IN YOUR CORRESPONDENCE

Recently, a friend texted me a question out of the blue: *Is anyone glamorous anymore?* My initial reaction was to say, *Yes, of course, just look at Zendaya in chain mail at the Met Gala. Look at Beyoncé's pregnancy photos. Look at Phoebe Waller-Bridge, holding her multiple Emmys and smoking a cigarette at the same time. Look at Natasha Lyonne, clomping around downtown Manhattan.* But the question continues to linger in my mind. Not to bring Merriam-Webster into this, but the dictionary definition of *glamour* is an "elusive, mysteriously exciting attractiveness." Perhaps what my friend meant was that people feel more accessible than ever before, at least on social media, and the elusiveness aspect of the word is eroding. Glamour involves an inexplicable need to tilt toward an inexplicable person or thing. It requires a bit of distance, a gap that can never be bridged.

In 1966, the Irish writer Maeve Brennan—who at the time had a sparkling column in the *New Yorker* magazine called "The Long-Winded Lady," in which she strolled around Manhattan and described eccentric strangers—took a long walk up Broadway on a hot summer evening. "To walk along Broadway," she wrote, "is like being a ticket in a lottery—a ticket in a glass barrel, being tossed about with all the other tickets. There are eyes everywhere." As Brennan flitted up the street, looking like a winning ticket herself—she was svelte and stylish, prone to wearing oversized spectacles and black sheath dresses; some say her friend Truman Capote poured many of her coltish

affectations into Holly Golightly—her eyes landed on another woman who seemed to her like nothing short of an apparition. "She wore a tight white crepe dress, much whiter than flesh, and she had a small fluffy white mink stole around her shoulders and her bosom," Brennan wrote. She noticed that the woman was carrying a transparent plastic handbag that contained only one tube of lipstick, "which rolled about like dice." This single lipstick baffled Brennan, transfixed her. It made her wonder if the woman was carrying any money—it certainly wasn't in her pocketbook—and, if so, where was it tucked away? And why was she wearing a fur stole in summertime, when the air in Manhattan feels thick enough to swallow? "We all stared at her, in our different ways," wrote Brennan. "And from our attention she drew the air of indifference that made her a star. She cast swift glances right and left to show us how she despised us all, and then she vanished, leaving us with nothing to look at except ourselves."

Brennan writes about this sultry stranger as if she were a sorceress or a ghost. She seems to appear and disappear in a puff of city steam. Why was she carrying *only* a lipstick anyway? Did she forget her keys? Was she even real? Was she keeping a wad of cash in her bra? "I kept thinking about the girl in the mink stole," Brennan writes at the end of her column—which often sounded like very decadent letters to the reader. "I wish I knew what her reason was."

Brennan never uses the term *glamorous* to describe this woman, but she did not have to. It is there, bubbling like good Champagne underneath this otherwise unremarkable urban encounter. Glamour is what happens when encounters tip into enchantments, when the mind starts to overflow its brim with both confusion and desire. Brennan couldn't stop thinking about the woman in the mink stole who seemed to vanish into thin air. As for me, lately I cannot seem to stop thinking about Maeve

The New Plaza Hotel, New York.

How to Maintain a Glamorous Mystique in Your Correspondence

Brennan, who never lived in one room for too long, though she lived in New York City for most of her adult life. She made her home in hotels and boardinghouses around the city, ate alone at diners more nights than not, cracked wise with her editors over stiff vodka stingers, and spent most of her time observing strangers at bars and restaurants while she sat in a corner with a notebook. She lived among her subjects; she drank with them, she feasted with them, she walked miles over the same city streets as they did. Unfortunately, her insistence on being as untethered as the city she wrote about began to catch up to her health. By the early seventies, Brennan was an alcoholic. Her eccentricities, which were once as translucent and shiny as the stranger's see-through purse, started to turn into heavy baggage. She began sleeping in the *New Yorker* offices, sometimes in the women's bathroom. By the 1980s, she, too, vanished from the street like the woman who fascinated her, leaving those in her orbit with nothing to look at except themselves. She briefly reappeared in a flophouse near Times Square in the nineties, and then finally died in a nursing home in Queens at only seventy-six years old.

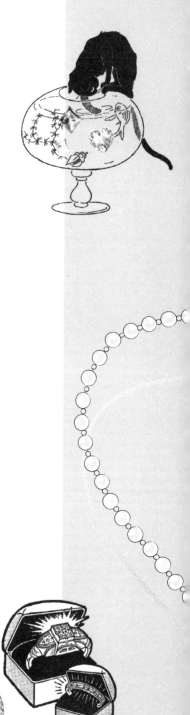

> Glamour is what happens when encounters tip into enchantments, when the mind starts to overflow its brim with both confusion and desire.

Brennan was a woman who lived beyond her means and, in so doing, overdrew on her emotional accounts. We can't know what exactly caused her to disappear, but the story captivates me because of these gaps: Would Brennan still be glamorous if she had survived the clarity with which she saw the city? Or is she glamorous precisely because she was trapped by her own schtick, left to wander the streets she once wrote dispatches about? Glamour leaves you guessing; it leaves behind a perfume trail.

In 1966, glamour looked like a mink stole on a confident stranger. But what does it look like now? What does glamour mean in the 2020s, and what is its function? The word itself feels like it has a patina on it, like it has been deadened from overuse in fashion magazines and Hollywood red carpet specials, in need of a good dusting off and shaking out through an open window.

The word *glamour* comes from the Scots English, from the same people who brought us all-butter shortbread and the Weird Sisters and plaid fabrics threaded with subtextual meanings. Sometime around the early 1700s, just before Scotland's Enlightenment and before the union with England that would transform the country from a rural misty dampness on the map into a wealthy industrial power, the Scots transformed the word *grammar* into something adjacent but far more elusive. If grammar had rules, glamour was the point at which the rules stopped making sense. *Glamour* meant mystery, alchemy, occult spells. To use it in a sentence: *The witch cast a glamour over me . . .* , meaning she did something that I do not understand but that has left me utterly changed and perhaps cursed.

Glamouring as a verb was always happening in mirrors—something showed up in the reflection that wasn't supposed to be there; a waifish specter, maybe, or a wispy smoke trail. The fear of glamour was a fear of being controlled by something totally outside of one's control; vampires could use glamour spells to captivate and distract their human targets before sinking their fangs into flesh. This phobia arose, as most phobias do, from a lack of doing the reading; most Scots in the late seventeenth century were largely illiterate (why would a cow farmer who tends only to the heath need any other text than the soil?), at least in the Latin they associated with *grimoire*, or texts written in antiquated languages with darkness and deception. Glamour was inscrutable, but it was seductive. It could ensorcell you and turn you into a bat. However, if you learned how to read it, and then to master it yourself, you could transcend yourself. If a person took an active interest in the Latin grammatica, which included subjects such as astrology and necromancy and herbal magick, they were not to be trusted, but they did command attention. Glamour was a power that came through study; it was, in those early days, about the fearsome power of being well-read. To glamour someone was to pull one over on them, maybe fantastically, maybe fatally. It was about being tricked by magic, lured into a trap, frozen in your tracks, dazzled by fog.

In the ornate 1800s, the meaning of *glamour* shifted slightly, though the root stayed the same. Glamour became synonymous with allure, with opulent beauty, with desire so palpable that it hurt your teeth, with untouchable, unobtainable things that nonetheless have a tangible, textural appeal. But it was also still a lie, a magic trick, a sleight-of-hand act. Glamour looked gilded and opulent, but it was also entirely human-made and perhaps a bit flimsy around the edges; it was silk gowns and velvet curtains and heavy maquillage.

By the time "Hollywood Glamour" came around in the early twentieth century, the precedent had already been set: Glamour was a gleaming and glittery false front that still managed to enthrall and entice people into changing their lives to possess it; nowhere was better equipped to engage in a large-scale public deception the way that the studio system was in early Hollywood. They built the backlots and then made cardboard and wheat paste look as solid as the pyramids. Everything in the movies was like that drawing that looks like a rabbit if you stare at it one way and a duck if you stare at it another—but, in this case, you only saw the fantasy the producers wanted you to see; they controlled the rabbits and the ducks.

This glamour, too, had its roots in grammar, in prescribed rules. It was a glamour designed to make desire mechanically reproducible: The stars of the studio era had to conform to type, to a dress size, to a hair color, to a lifetime role as the vamp or the rogue, the comic relief or the ingenue. This is why, when we look

photos of Rudolph Valentino or Lillian Gish, there is a sad patina to them; these were people trapped in amber during their own lifetimes. If we see the glamour in their lives still, it is in what we imagine was happening far off-screen; the pool parties where people danced naked in the moonlight, the jaguars kept as house cats, the heavy sateen robes and marabou powder puffs, the smell of tuberose perfume on a vanity.

We look at these pictures and free these stars from their burdens in our heads; sure, they were kept on horrible contracts that violated their privacy and their ability to live honestly in public, but we perform the magic trick of imagining them as libertines, as grandiose.

That's what glamour does: It shows you the rules and lets you apply the magic yourself, as if filling in a paint-by-numbers image. You see a fur coat and instantly picture the woman who would inhabit it, walking down a Manhattan boulevard on a frosty afternoon. You see a diamond pendant and think of the neck it will adorn. You see a placid, curaçao-blue pool and think of the bodies breaking its surface. Glamour is about filling in gaps—vaulting yourself into other lives, other places, other clothes. In that sense it has never lost its original connection to spells and incantations; to consider something glamorous is to stare at it long enough that it is transformed and becomes more than what it was before. Glamour, like the grammatica it derives from, invites you to read.

The few letters we have by Maeve Brennan currently sit in a library in Atlanta in a locked archive. She remains elusive, even now. But I encourage you to channel her in your letter-writing—remain breathlessly curious about others, but also leave room in your own letters for a bit of mystery and intrigue. Mention some fabulous trip you took in a single sentence and then never mention it again. Drop a line about a new love affair without revealing too much. Make grand pronouncements and dangle sumptuous stories without finishing them. It might be maddening, but you should sometimes leave your reader wanting more. You can be anyone you want to be in a letter. Maybe, today, you're Greta Garbo.

How to Maintain a Glamorous Mystique in Your Correspondence

Get into it:
Fountain Pens

If you were to run into me on the street, on any given day, chances are I am going to have a giant ink stain on my right middle finger. The color might change—these days, my fingertips are persimmon orangey-red because I am powering through a gorgeous bottle of Pilot Iroshizuku ink in "Fuyu-gaki"; last month they were stained the sparkly Aegean blue of Birmingham Pen Company's "Polar Bear" ink—but the smudges remain constant.

I don't seem to be able to use a fountain pen without some of its contents bleeding into my skin, and as I am always using fountain pens, I more or less live with a semi-permanent, blobby tattoo at all times. I barely notice it anymore, as it is such a transient marking—the stains always wash away after a few baths or dishwashing sessions, and if I really need to make them disappear, I use a nail scrubber and some baking soda—but I also like the fact that I bear the signs of a person who still writes by hand.

More than once, while I have been reporting a story, the subject will notice my hand and ask me about it, and soon we are tossing back and forth our favorite pen models and rummaging around in our bags to pull out a Lamy Al-star or Pilot Falcon to show off. Once you start talking about your fountain pens, I have found, it turns out you will find enthusiasts *everywhere*.

Fountain pens are easy to love and even easier to feel irrationally passionate about. Because they feel both timeless and also distinctly from another time, you always have a hunch that you are the first person to discover them, or at least to bring them back into fashion. And somehow this feeling of rarefied specialness is not at all diminished by the fact that

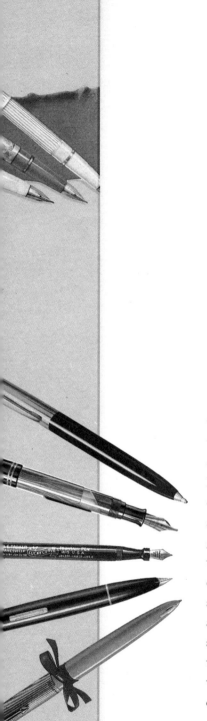

this may be the best time in history to get into fountain pens, as there are so many rabid nib fans and retail sellers and vintage pen vendors out there, all swapping knowledge (and vehement opinions). While this may not be the era of Peak Pen, in which every business titan kept a heavy Esterbrook gold nib in a display stand on top of a hulking wooden desk, we are in a new and more open kind of golden age. It has never been cheaper, simpler, or less complicated to dip your toe into the inkwell of fountain pen mania (of course, things can quickly get expensive and complex—how far you want to get into the hobby is entirely up to you, as there is no real end point).

The fountain pen is a constantly evolving tool, even now. Legend has it that Leonardo da Vinci made one of his own design back in the 1500s, but they did not become well-known until the early nineteenth century. They did not become really usable (as in, without causing extreme leakage or contending with scratchy, unstable nibs) until the late nineteenth century, and they did not attain mainstream popularity until the mid-twentieth century. To qualify as a fountain pen, a pen must technically have three parts—a body, a reservoir (or a cartridge) that holds ink inside said body, and a nib into which the ink flows. How the ink makes its way from the barrel to the nib is a bit different for each pen, but it generally works as a kind of purposeful, regulated leaking, in which gravity causes ink to flow downward, while small channels in the pen cause air to flow upward and create a vacuum-like seal, keeping the ink from dribbling out at all times. The process only gets more intricate from there, and, as such, I tend to leave my fountain pen repairs to the professionals. (If you are in New York City, you can visit the Fountain Pen Hospital in Manhattan to have a leaky or squeaky pen fixed, or you can ship them your hobbled Parker 51 from anywhere.) Keeping your pen well-lubricated, regularly cleaned and serviced, and in fighting form is half the fun of owning one. Rare are the objects that we buy for life; fountain pens—at least those that begin with solid construction—can last for decades, and even centuries, if you care for them.

127

How to Maintain a Glamorous Mystique in Your Correspondence

My own love affair with fountain pens began three years ago. I had owned stately pens before—like many girls who had Bat Mitzvahs before me, someone gave me a Cross ballpoint that I promptly lost before I hit high school, and I received a lovely slim eggshell blue Tiffany rollerball in my twenties as the prize for winning an award for fragrance journalism—but I had always been afraid of fountain pens. They seemed too persnickety, too messy, too prone to breaking down or drying out. I had played around with them in my late grandfather's study when I was young, and I remembered finding them heavy and intimidating. When I report a story, I always use a Uniball roller pen, which costs $3 and lasts forever. I did not want to bother with the fuss of traveling around with a fountain pen—the extra ink vials, the leakproof carrying case, the blotting paper for wiping down the nib. It all felt very *effortful*.

And, then, I started writing letters. When you write letters, at least by hand, you want your pen to feel as eventful as your correspondence. The fuss of the fountain pen can become part of the daily desk ritual if you take the time to enjoy it: the flushing out of old ink to make way for the influx of the new, the loopy practice strokes to get the flow going, the care you must put into not smearing the wet, glossy ink as it streams from your hand. My gateway pen was a piston-filler TWSBI Diamond 580 with a medium nib that I ordered late one night from the online retailer Goulet Pens (just one of many great fountain pen sellers online—see the shoppies list on page 111 for more!). I paired it with a well of Jacques Herbin ink in Émeraude de Chivor—a brilliant blue-green the color of a peacock feather—and marveled as the pen suctioned up the liquid with one twist of my hand. The pen (which I still use today) glided quickly over the page like a figure skater preparing for a triple Lutz. It felt as substantial and useful in my hand as a steel soup spoon. I was hooked. I was in trouble.

In the years since, I have acquired almost thirty pens (yikes!) from various eras and at various price points. I have entry-level Pilot Metropolitans and Lamy Safaris, a slim vintage Sheaffer Ladies' Pen (see page 134 for more on that gem), work-

"It has never been cheaper, simpler, or less complicated to dip your toe into the inkwell of fountain pen mania."

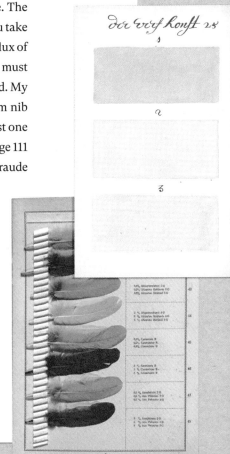

horse pens (my Pilot Vanishing Point, my Conklin Duragraph), and the splurge-y dream pen I saved up for—my Pilot Custom 823, which I love and cherish like a piece of fine jewelry. I have found, via trial and error, that I like a broad, flex nib best (I am what pen-heads call a "wet writer"; I like a thick, slick line) and that I like to "post" my pens while writing, an industry term for popping the pen cap onto the back of the pen like a little hat. But the glory of fountain pens is that there are endless options.

You might be into ultra-fine nibs! Japanese pen engineering! Aluminum barrels! Duochrome shimmer inks! 14K gold stub nibs from Italy!

So consider your letter-writing a ready excuse to dive into the wild and weird and whimsical world of fountain-penning. There is so much to explore, and so many inks to sample.

How to Maintain a Glamorous Mystique in Your Correspondence

SINCERELY CONSIDER . . .

Ink Samples

Did you know that you don't have to buy a full bottle of fountain pen ink to try out a new color?! This was a revelation to me and I pass it along to you. Online retailers like Goulet and Goldspot, as well as several sellers on Etsy, offer sample vials of ink that go for under $5 and let you fill up at least one full barrel. I recently went on a hunt for the perfect shade of hot pink and ordered five nearly identical ink samples; I found that in practice, they were wildly different. One was watery and thin, one stuck to my nib like syrup, and another looked bright on the bottle but came out a pale peony color that was impossible to read. I found the perfect fit (Herbin Rose Cyclamen), but only through this Goldilocks process. Ink is a rabbit hole to catapult yourself down, but it is nice to know that you can try before you get in too deep.

How to Embrace the Penternet

The *New York Times* ran a feature in its Styles section called, "What Killed Penmanship?" noting that in the age of texting and typing and asking Siri to fetch us our search results, good, old-fashioned handwriting has gone extinct. There is always a bit of a pearl-clutch to articles like these, as if somehow the very fabric of civilization is being held together by the thinnest of thread (and that thread is knowing how to write out a proper uppercase "G" in cursive), but handwritten communication is, if not currently on its last legs, definitely hobbling. It is gradually becoming an antiquated, peculiar thing, like watch fobs or opera goggles or cigarette cases; you can be *into* it, certainly, but then you will become known as the kind of person who is into it.

Having good penmanship now is not a prerequisite for getting through the third grade; it is an entire personality. It is a calling. You don't *need* it to make it in business (when was the last time you had to write out a work communiqué?) or even in polite society. Paperless Post wedding invitations, for example, are easier, more sustainable, and far less expensive than the paper alternative. (Pour those funds into the honeymoon!) They do still teach script in school, but most students eagerly ditch their pencils for a laptop as soon as their parents or the school will allow. If you want to maintain your handwriting past middle school, you really have to work at it. You have to practice daily. You have to keep your pen-holding hand loose and limber so you don't get a palm cramp after two sentences. You have to make peace with developing unseemly writing calluses that will lend your otherwise dainty, computer-pampered hands a slightly grotesque, ogress quality. And, perhaps more than anything, you have to become a *maniac* about your writing tools.

As penmanship has moved from a foundational skill to a fringe fetish over the years, so, too, have writing implements splintered off into niches, inspiring separate-but-equally-devoted camps of highly opinionated fanatics who live to nerd out over graphite lead or stub nibs or ballpoint width or the viscosity of walnut ink. If handwriting is experiencing a small surge in popularity among a

Embrace the Penternet?   Ignore

new generation, it is not because it is a newly vital medium—it is because there are just so many ways now to obsess. I, for one, welcome this vast online chirography universe; it is not killing the ancient art of putting pen to paper, but trying to infuse it with new life. If handwriting stands a chance, it is going to be because the burgeoning pen geeks out there are pumping it with fresh blood (or, more accurately, with oxblood ink).

One of my favorite places on earth (or at least on the Internet) is the r/Fountainpens subreddit, a wooly thicket of penheads posting daily about recent purchases, nib hacks, fresh ink colors, holy grail vintage models, and every other nerdy little thing you can think of. Beyond Reddit, you can find the soothing world of ink swatch blogs (where someone will write with and compare every shade of turquoise ink on the market), breathless fountain pen reviews on YouTube, live-streaming handwriting courses, practice sheets you can print on demand, cursive influencers who peddle their own brands of nib holders and inkwells and whose ornate lettering flourishes garner hundreds of thousands of likes on Instagram, and TikTok feeds dedicated to unboxing and writing with pens for the first time. If you want to get really wonky, you can join the Fountain Pen Network, an old-school Web 1.0–style message board full of pen geeks at their most ardent and compulsive, though newbies beware: That board is not for the faint of heart (I noped out after being yelled at for not knowing what a music nib was). Fountain pens no longer exist in a time capsule; a teeming ecosystem has sprung up around keeping them in the public conversation. The penternet is the one corner of the web that always makes me want to get off of it and do something tactile.

SINCERELY
CONSIDER . . .

Getting lost in #mailart Instagram

Letter writing is not immune to online discourse. Wherever you find your scrolling content, you can surely locate a vibrant corner of the platform devoted to correspondence-adjacent posts. On Instagram, the #mailart hashtag is a goldmine; I have lost hours of my life swiping through wildly creative envelopes embellished with lace and glitter and stamp art and even . . . doll hair? It is so heartening to see that so many of the biggest accounts on #mailart Instagram are teenagers who have created their own online communities dedicated to sending one another sumptuous mail; nobody bedazzles a letter better than a teen with a glue gun.

Cancel

OK

Fountain Pens: Vintage or New?

The question that awaits every fledgling fountain pen lover: Should my next pen be a vintage find or a new model? Chances are you will end up with one of each if the hobby catches your spirit, but for the sake of promoting healthy debate, here is a little list to guide your decision.

Vintage Pens

Your pen will have a backstory—or at least a backstory that you can invent. I like to imagine some Joan Holloway wearing my Lady Sheaffer around her neck like a pendant as she clomped around the office.

Dubious eBay sellers can lead to heartbreak (though there are also wonderful sellers who refurbish every vintage pen with loving care and deep knowledge).

One-of-a-kind, collectors' items that nobody else will have.

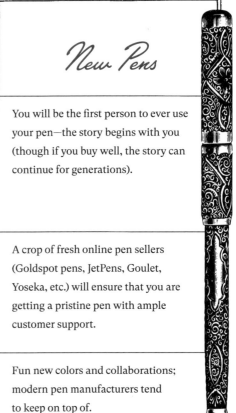

New Pens

You will be the first person to ever use your pen—the story begins with you (though if you buy well, the story can continue for generations).

A crop of fresh online pen sellers (Goldspot pens, JetPens, Goulet, Yoseka, etc.) will ensure that you are getting a pristine pen with ample customer support.

Fun new colors and collaborations; modern pen manufacturers tend to keep on top of.

Vintage Pens

In order to really understand what to buy, you must speak, regularly and often, with vintage pen experts (a rare and eccentric breed) and visit eclectic shops like the Fountain Pen Hospital in Manhattan or Penfriend in London if your model breaks. Depending on your enjoyment when it comes to speaking to strangers, this may be your idea of heaven or hell.

Often pricey, but sometimes totally worth it. And sometimes absolutely insane . . . how can a pen cost more than a studio apartment???

Elegant! A conversation piece! If someone asks, you can say, "Oh, this old thing? This is a vintage Montegrappa. The kind that Hemingway used."

Many argue that fountain pens used to be better (AKA the "They simply don't make 'em like they used to" camp). Iconic vintage pens, like the original, famous Parker 51 from the 1940s or a Waterman 55 from the 1920s, were built to last centuries.

New Pens

Every new pen to market comes with many amateur reviews (see the section on the Penternet, page 130). You'll find oodles of information about each model out there, so you can research what to buy without ever having to set foot in a store. That said, there are new stores where you can try out new pens and speak to experts.

Many price points, especially on the lower, beginner end. I never recommend going under $20 (disposable fountain pens like the Pilot Varsity tend to break after just a few uses), but there are so many great pens for under $100.

You can get exactly what you want. What you lose in a tall tale, you gain in being able to customize.

Technology has come a long way! New pens are often easier to fill, easier to clean, and easier to maintain than their vintage counterparts. They require less up-front maintenance and are ready to use right out of the box.

The History
of the Ladies' Pen

In March of 1958, fifty years after a businessman from Iowa named Walter Sheaffer patented the first-ever lever-fill fountain pen, the W.A. Sheaffer Pen Company debuted the "Lady Sheaffer," the first pen of its kind marketed specifically as a fashion accessory for women. The media roll-out for the pen was grand—this was the golden age of advertising, and the mark of some maverick Don Draper type is all over it— with a special press preview for editors of *Vogue* and *Mademoiselle* and a national print ad campaign that ran in every women's fashion magazine as well as the *New Yorker*, *Life*, and *Reader's Digest*. The Lady Sheaffer also made an appearance at the 1958 World's Fair in Brussels as an innovation in writing instruments—though, really, all it is is a skinny fountain pen that comes in pretty colors with metallic accents and its own little carrying case.

In recent years, I have found myself drawn to the Lady Sheaffer (often called a Sheaffer "Skripsert"), not because it is a particularly great pen—I have a pink and silver beauty that I bought on eBay, and it is frustratingly inconsistent despite many tune-ups; I think of it now more as a desk decoration—but because it is so daffy an idea. A dainty pen . . . for women's wee little hands! The tagline, WRITES LIKE A DREAM, REFILLS LIKE HER LIPSTICK! is so exactly the kind of tagline that a man who has never held a tube of lipstick in his life writes about what women want.

The 1958 Sheaffer catalog—which I can only assume was also written by a man—boasts that "It is the first complete assortment of writing instruments to be engineered and designed expressly for women, and it is the first that has ever qualified for promotion and sale in the fashion accessory field." Note that it was not engineered *by* women, but for them, and that it allegedly doubles as a piece of jewelry. Who needs a diamond when you can have a Skripsert, ladies! The catalog goes on to read:

> Patterns for the Lady Sheaffer collection are taken from fine fabrics, including tweed, corduroy, paisley, tulle, moire, brocade, spun silver, petit point, damask and matelasse. Many models have decorative bands and brilliants. Nibs are available in medium, fine, shorthand and extra fine gradations. They feature easy filling, using Skrip cartridges. Packaging for the Lady Sheaffer pens is as different as the product itself. They will be displayed and sold in high-fashion gift boxes of gray suede finish, much like that now used for precious perfumes. A purse case for the pen and a matching pouch for a reserve supply of Skrip cartridges are included with every model. They are made in 11 contemporary, matching fabrics. The pens have no clip, since Sheaffer research showed that women prefer not to have them, but the purse cases are designed to clip inside a purse, on a writing pad, in a note book, a pocket, to a belt or on a desk calendar pad.

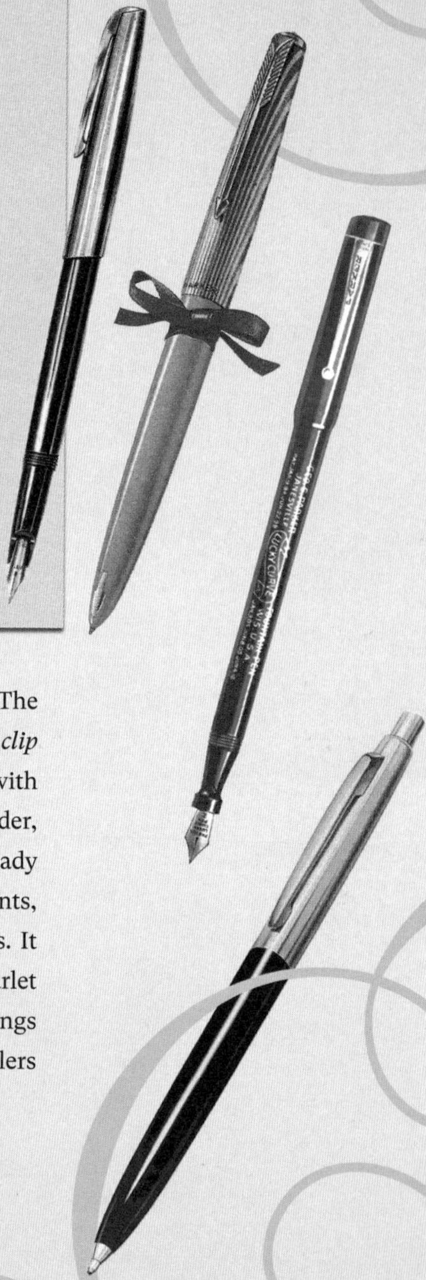

Damask and matelassé! A pen that comes in a perfume box! The fact that women have no use for something as pedestrian as a *pocket clip* (this was during the tyrannical age when no women's clothing came with pockets). It never goes near an ink bottle so you can keep your tender, flimsy, useless hands from incurring even a drop of damage! The Lady Sheaffer is so completely born out of the *idea* of what a woman wants, rather than what she really needs, that I find it irresistibly hilarious. It is high femininity as its most put-on and camp; it is stilettos and scarlet lipstick and false eyelashes. It is tuberose perfume and fishnet stockings and "Oops, I broke a nail!" It is a pen in full Texas drag. It is hot rollers and tulle and cold cream.

20 WEST 70TH ST   NEW YORK CITY

How to Write a Love Letter

Love letters are the blockbusters of the correspondence world. We've all heard about and read the famous ones; we've all read Shakespearean tragedies in school that hinge on ardent letters going missing or that turn on a besotted phrase between star-crossed lovers. Héloïse and Abelard, one of the first celebrity couples (due to their hot correspondence that later leaked to the public), were waxing to one another about the "maxims of Divine love" in Latin in medieval twelfth-century France (she was a precocious teenager who fell for her philosophy tutor and had a baby with him before her father shipped her off to a convent and castrated her paramour). If you google FAMOUS LOVE LETTERS, you will get thousands of results; they are practically postal memes at this point.

Because love letters are so widely published, you can easily find examples of every varietal of passion. Want dramatic, desperate devotion? Try Beethoven's letters to his "Immortal Beloved," who many think was the daughter of a foreign diplomat (Beethoven's sign-off, "Ever thine. Ever mine. Ever ours." has become so well-known that it was a major plot point in the *Sex and the City* movie.). Want gentle, flowing lustiness? Try the five thousand letters between the painter Georgia O'Keeffe and her husband, the photographer Alfred Stieglitz. (O'Keeffe: "I wonder if your body wants mine the way mine wants yours.") Want absolutely nasty, horndog smut? Look for the letters between James Joyce and his wife Nora. (Joyce: "Goodnight, my little farting Nora, my dirty little fuckbird!" . . . and that's just what is suitable to share here.) Want queer entanglement and high drama? Go for the correspondence between Oscar Wilde and his lover, Lord Alfred Douglas, whom he called "Bosie" and "my dearest boy." But while you can find countless collections of love letters to read, you will never truly understand, at least from the outside, what they are all about. Love letters are our most overexposed form of correspondence and also our most emotionally illegible.

You can never truly understand a love letter from someone else's relationship, just as you can never truly know what someone else's marriage is like. There are too many invisible signals, too much shared history, too private a vocabulary for a casual reader to ever really know what is happening between the lines. The love letters of strangers provide only a hazy glimpse into what a relationship was; all of its chaotic wobbles and moments of diamond hardness; the sicknesses and the health. That said, we keep reading them anyway, peering inside others' heartfelt dispatches looking for clues—about how to love another person, about how to express that love, and about how to keep that love alive even as time and distance threaten to erode it.

We still all write love letters in some form, when in those early throes of infatuation—they may be love texts, or love DMs, and they are all part of a grand tradition—but what has faded, despite our cultural obsession with the note d'amour, is the letter that comes midway through a relationship, when the spark has begun to fade. Sure, you might write a Valentine's card, but when is the last time you sat down and really wrote a *love* letter? A letter that told another person all of the things that keep you choosing to love them every day—because what is love if not a daily choice—just because you felt moved to do it? Maybe we are so entranced by vintage love letters because they feel like a relic of something we have lost; the overflowing of emotion on a random Tuesday, so much so that you are moved to write it down.

My suggestion: Write more love letters. Write them all the time. If you are not in a relationship, write them to your friends. Make them filthy if you want, or florid, or flirtatious. Make them full of sweeping declarations and lists of memories. Make a crossword puzzle just for one person. Send a selection of ephemera that you saved over the last year of being together with reminders about the significance of each piece. Send bad poetry. Leave the letter underneath someone's pillow. Or

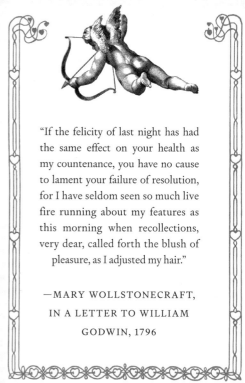

"If the felicity of last night has had the same effect on your health as my countenance, you have no cause to lament your failure of resolution, for I have seldom seen so much live fire running about my features as this morning when recollections, very dear, called forth the blush of pleasure, as I adjusted my hair."

—MARY WOLLSTONECRAFT,
IN A LETTER TO WILLIAM
GODWIN, 1796

drop it in the mail, even if it is coming right back to your address. Just because you see one another all the time does not mean you cannot write a letter full of yearning.

I am not inside your love, so I cannot tell you what to write. You can study the letters of the greats, of course, but they cannot tell you, either. All I know is that a love letter of any kind is a sacred and timeless object. It's one of the best vehicles humans have come up with for trying to put words to the ineffable.

HOW TO WRITE
ABOUT SECRETS

(OR THE ART OF VERY JUICY GOSSIP)

In early 2022, the journalist and author Kelsey McKinney and the audio producer Alex Sujong Laughlin launched a podcast called "Normal Gossip," in which they invite guests to discuss and investigate the low-stakes, mostly harmless rumors that have been swirling around their social circles—such as a lavish wedding gone sideways, high drama in a local kickball league, infighting among ruthless preschool parents, or a knitting club torn asunder by a rogue antivaxxer. The show was an instant hit; as it turns out, *everyone* loves to eavesdrop on hot goss, particularly when it involves petty, innocuous scuttlebutt about strangers you will never meet. My favorite way to inhale episodes is during long walks with the dog around the city; he sniffs, I dig my nose into decadent morsels of information that are truly none of my business.

"Good gossip feels *fizzy*, you know?" McKinney said in one interview about the show's addictive qualities. "Like when you shake a bottle of Coke and then open it up—that kind of energy that just explodes and overflows."

If you dive into letters of the past—from the pre-podcasting era—you will find that many of them are overflowing with bubbly, breathless bavardage. Letters were, for a time, *the* marquee medium for communicating unconfirmed rumors and slipped scandals. They offered a sense of privacy that allowed for open speculating and kvetching, but they also encouraged the writer to send their most entertaining and high-value information in order to keep the reader engaged in a bawdy back-

and-forth—as anyone who has passed a note in class can attest, a piece of paper containing a burning bit of information quickly becomes prized property.

While, these days, it is a wise idea never to put anything in writing that you wouldn't want to see pop up elsewhere, many longtime letter writers saw their correspondence as a joint and inviolable social contract: You tell me your secrets, I'll tell you mine, and we will tuck these papers away from prying eyes until death do us part. (Much of the best historical gossip does come out when a posthumous archive goes public; if you're buried, you can't be too upset about what gets unearthed.) Sure, there is still always a small risk when sending off a hunk of hearsay—the letter could, theoretically, fall into the wrong hands and create chaos—but life rarely contains such farcical twists. The mutual understanding that letters are sacrosanct spaces for dishing is perhaps more relevant now than it has ever been; there is an unspoken rule that anything that comes in an envelope demands much more care than what you might toss around at a party after a few Manhattans or even over email or text (I personally consider group text threads to be utterly sacred, but you never know).

As for the guilt: Unburden yourself. Letters are not newspaper columns; you're not Walter Winchell out to burn up someone's life with scalding tea. Unless you are accusing someone of a crime or admitting that you plan to commit one, handwritten gossip tends to be harmless and maybe even healthy. We all need to get it out somewhere. While the Nobel Prize–winning scientist Marie Curie allegedly once said that one should "be less curious about people and more curious about ideas," you should see your letters as a place where you can explore everything you are curious about, even if it is how your two coworkers—who may or may not be having an affair—are managing the drama on top of their deadlines or why your local bodega seems to be in a vicious turf war with the fruit stand across the street (also, that Marie Curie quote might not even be real! Many scholars believe it to be a . . . gasp . . . unverified rumor that has made its way to inspirational Instagram feeds and Etsy mugs).

Gossip is, at heart, a form of active perception, of putting together hunches and observations and, yes, even *ideas*, and swirling them together into sentences. The way we dish is the way we are; if you do it with a sense of nimble lightness, rather than pettiness and misanthropy, it will pop off the page.

To keep your letters tart, vivacious, and compulsively readable, I advise sticking to the three cardinal rules of good correspondence dish:

1. **KEEP IT LOW-STAKES (AND PREFERABLY ABOUT PEOPLE YOUR CORRESPONDENT DOES NOT KNOW).**
One of the benefits of writing letters to someone in another state or another country is that they have *no* clue about the manager you work with who has been causing endless chaos at work, or the woman whose dog keeps peeing on your neighbor's lawn leading to a cul-de-sac battle, or the friend of a friend who is having a wild tryst with a B-list celebrity. Some of the best letters I've ever received have been pages-long sagas that read like Edith Wharton novels about characters I will never encounter and never hope to—I still think about a five-page letter I got from one of my regular pen pals about a woman who had intimidated her since graduate school and became her professional nemesis—until the woman became embroiled in a thorny local *scandale* when she blew up her marriage to start dating a powerful city official. It had twists! Turns! A sidenote in a local paper that my pen pal ripped out and included as evidence! A letter to a far-off reader is a perfect place to put an epic tale of intrigue about something ridiculous.

WHISPER AWAY!

2. **IF YOU CAN, BE NEUTRAL, OR AT LEAST BE FUNNY.** In his play, *Lady Windemere's Fan*, Oscar Wilde has a character named Sir Cecil Graham say, "My dear Arthur, I never talk scandal, I only talk gossip." When Arthur presses Cecil to explain the difference, Cecil goes on: "Oh! Gossip is charming! History is merely gossip. But scandal is gossip made tedious by morality." Don't make your gossip tedious by imposing your own pearl-clutching or side-eye onto it; what will be most charming about a rumor-filled letter is the sparkling little details, not the sense that you are here to cast aspersions. Instead, ask yourself why you found a story delicious enough to repeat: Is it bizarre? Is it mysterious? Is it so gross or embarrassing or unbelievable that it comes back around the horn and becomes hysterical? In other words: If you are not as entertaining in the telling as the story is, then it isn't worth putting in a letter.

3. **BE COLORFUL.** It's all about the details. Epistolary gossip is best when you can get really granular with it. Describe the REPLY ALL email chain at work that went totally off the rails or the dysfunctional family wedding that imploded with discrete descriptions of each person involved (I've even been known to draw a flowchart once or twice). Think of yourself as a raconteur holding court on a velvet divan while sucking on a long cigarette-holder. People come to sit at your feet and hear tales—of deceit, of romantic dalliance, of jealousy and sabotage and desire and ambition. Do not disappoint your audience.

How to Write about Secrets

Emboss, Baby

I am not, despite my love of paper goods, what one might consider a "crafty" person. I don't knit, or weave, or quilt, or scrapbook. Every Sculpey bead I made growing up cracked and disintegrated as soon as I could thread it onto a hemp necklace (nineties kids were a generation bombarded with cheesy craft projects). I am, however, a lover of crafting *supplies*; I never met a jar of glitter or a bolt of calico fabric or a pair of scalloped scissors that I didn't want to lug home with me from JOANN's.

Most of these tools end up in a box somewhere, half-used and half-loved, but there is one goofy crafting tool that will likely stick with me for years to come: my embossing wand. I love the way embossing looks on the paper: textured, gleamy, effortlessly elegant. As it turns out, an embossing wand is simply a glorified, powerful little blow-dryer that blasts scalding air out of the tip and generally costs less than $40. Add a rubber stamp of your choosing, embossing powder, embossing glue, and a good YouTube tutorial, and you will be gilding all of your letters in no time.

Here is the simple method I use:

1. **PICK** out a **RUBBER STAMP** you would like to use as an embossed image. Bold, graphic stamps work better than very detailed ones, but I've embossed nearly every stamp in my collection and they all work in some form.

2. **PRESS** the stamp into a pad of **CLEAR EMBOSSING GLUE.** You can find these pads in craft stores and online; I swear by the Tsukineko VersaMark pad.

3. **STAMP** the image onto a sheet of paper or an envelope. The glue will be clear but shiny, so you can see where you placed the image. Tap out a pile

Syme's Letter Writer

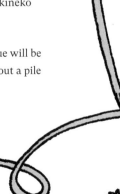

of **EMBOSSING POWDER** onto the image, covering it completely. This should look like a wee ant hill; be generous with your pour, as you can save the excess to reuse.

4. **FORM** a funnel with the paper and pour any excess powder back into the container, and then lightly tap the paper on a hard surface to shake off any errant powder that is not clinging to the image. Some people use a brush for this step to gingerly sweep away rogue flakes, but I find this fussy and I never do it.

5. **THE FUN PART:** Plug in your **EMBOSSING WAND** and turn it on HIGH, bringing it close to the powder-caked image but not touching it; blow the hot air on a diagonal (from about an inch or so away) across the image. Like magic, the powder will instantly melt and bond to the glue and the image will snap into sharp focus. You are done when no dark powder remains (be sure to stop right when this happens, as you don't want to further melt the glue).

6. **CONGRATS,** you are now addicted to embossing. It was inevitable.

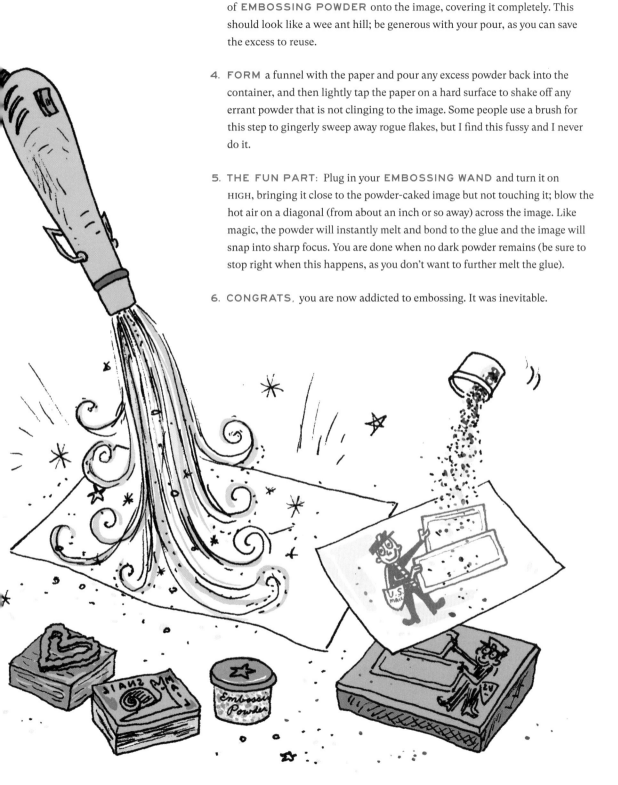

HOW TO WRITE
A BITCHY LETTER

(OR THE ART OF THE POISON PEN)

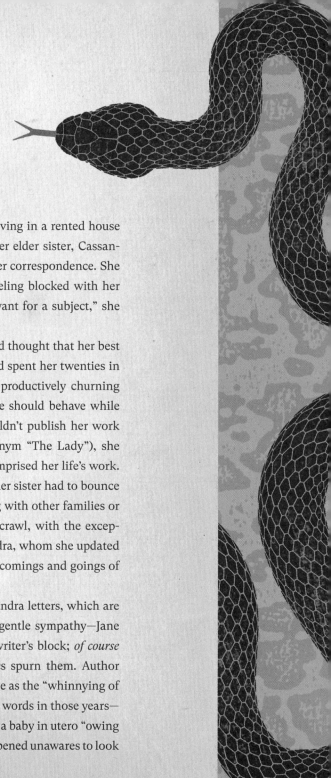

In 1807, when she was thirty-one years old and living in a rented house in Southampton, Jane Austen wrote a letter to her elder sister, Cassandra, apologizing for being so sharp-tongued in her correspondence. She veered into venom, she said, because she was feeling blocked with her own writing. "I am forced to be abusive out of want for a subject," she wrote, "having nothing really to say."

At the time, Austen was feeling frustrated and thought that her best compositional years might be behind her. She had spent her twenties in the bucolic Hampshire cottage she grew up in, productively churning out novels about love and manners and how one should behave while wearing an empire-waist dress. Though she wouldn't publish her work until the 1810s (anonymously, using the pseudonym "The Lady"), she carried with her the stack of manuscripts that comprised her life's work. After Austen's father died, Jane, her mother, and her sister had to bounce around to various run-down homes, often staying with other families or in temporary lodgings. Her writing slowed to a crawl, with the exception of a steady stream of letters, many to Cassandra, whom she updated with spiky and petulant details about the various comings and goings of her days.

Many Austen scholars tend to view the Cassandra letters, which are often barbed and even viperous, with a kind of gentle sympathy—Jane was childless, without property, suffering from writer's block; *of course* she was going to be on edge—while some critics spurn them. Author E. M. Forster dismissed the sororal correspondence as the "whinnying of harpies." Austen did scribble out some truly harsh words in those years— she quipped to Cassandra after a local woman lost a baby in utero "owing to fright" that the scare likely came when "she happened unawares to look

at her husband"—but most of her comments were harmless jeers about dull social visits and benign faux pas. She recognized, also, that her biting tone came mostly out of self-pity. In that 1807 letter, after she mocks a widower for thinking that he can do better in his second marriage than "his daughter's governess," she admitted that she was in a stormy

mood, turning her inward vexation into cheap shots at others. "We are cold here," she ended her letter, a weather update that seemed to carry a double meaning. "I expect a severe March, a wet April, and a sharp May."

Now that two hundred–plus years have passed, Austen's meanest letters no longer carry much of a sting. They have passed into the public domain and into legend; flinty prose smoothed out and polished to a sheen over time. Sometimes, you just need to write a letter full of vinegar, even if it is because you don't really have anything else to say. What is developing a private, cone-of-trust correspondence for if not the permission to be a whinnying harpy for a few lines without judgment from the other end? I have a friend who always texts me with the line, "Can I be a huge bitch for a second?" before sending along some savory, devastating opinion, and my answer is always, "Yes, of course." All is forgiven (and for the most part, never spoken of again) between friends in the sacred bubble of late-night texting, and so it shall be in your letters. Better out than in!

Teddy Roosevelt's daughter, Alice Roosevelt Longworth, reportedly kept a pillow in her sitting room embroidered with the phrase, "If you don't have anything nice to say, come sit right here by me." If you are concerned about being too acidic in your correspondence, try to channel Alice a little bit. A letter can be a cozy couch where you curl up to honor the words on that pillow. You will, at the least, be joining a grand tradition of writers who didn't hold back.

There is an art to sending a poison-pen letter, of course. Wit is always better than wanton meanness. Also: The people or situations you dislike say as much about who you are as they do the object of your ire, so know that you are really writing about yourself when you grumble. Whoever is reading your letter will forever view the surliest sentence you ever write in light of what they know about you. Think of deploying cattiness in your letters like tweezing an errant eyebrow hair: Go in surgically, yank quickly, and move on.

In a letter that has been floating around the Internet for years, the actress Joan Crawford, who was engaged in a cold war of mutual dislike with her *Whatever Happened to Baby Jane?* costar Bette Davis, allegedly wrote the film's director asking him to "talk to Bette about her body odor," and adds, "I have found myself gagging on several occasions during this filming." Whether the letter is real or not has been much debated among Old Hollywood scholars; one of Crawford's past assistants insists that it is authentic and written on her stationery, others believe it to be a clever piece of fan fiction or an Internet hoax. But the letter certainly *feels* true, in that Crawford was a notorious battle-ax (the kind of staunch woman an old-time gossip columnist might call a "harridan") and was not shy about voicing her dissatisfaction with her costars. She very publicly said of Bette Davis that "She has a cult, and what the hell is a cult except a gang of rebels without a cause? I have fans. There's a big difference." So it would

not be shocking that she continued her campaign in her private correspondence. But, real or not, the letter about B.O. is *beloved*, perhaps because it is so brutal and unapologetic that it nearly becomes high comedy. That's the thing about a bitchy letter—and Crawford famously said, "There's a lot of bitch in every woman"—it has to be smart, and it has to be fun to read. If you're going to be wicked, do it with panache.

Si on pouvait couper ta langue de serpent.

forging someone else's letter style to find your own

One of the great New York movies of the past decade is Marielle Heller's *Can You Ever Forgive Me?*, adapted from Lee Israel's memoir of the same name. In it, Melissa McCarthy plays Leonore "Lee" Israel, a struggling, hard-drinking, cantankerous middle-aged author whose showbusiness biographies don't sell and whose agent won't return her phone calls. She lives in the Upper West Side in the 1990s, but her world is a far cry from Nora Ephron's cozy literary scene; Israel was lonesome and misanthropic, the kind of person to steal an expensive coat from a book party. After losing her job, she becomes increasingly desperate for money and, after learning that there is a market for rare archival letters written by famous authors, turns her journalistic talents to crafting epistolary forgeries.

Israel turned out to be a gifted copycat; she bought old typewriters and churned out fake letters by Dorothy Parker, Noël Coward, and Ernest Hemingway, among others. In many cases, the letters were so charming and so evocative of the writers Israel was parroting that scholars put them in library archives and in museum exhibitions.

Israel was later convicted of fraud, served six months under house arrest, and was permanently banned from visiting archives and libraries, but her scamming spree raises interesting questions about authorship: If the forgery is as good as or better than the original, does it have artistic merit? I am not suggesting that you commit white-collar crimes. I do think, however, that it can be a good exercise to step up your correspondence game by attempting to write a letter like someone else.

Keep a copy of *Joan Crawford: Her Life in Letters* near your desk if you are looking to improve your barbed insults. Turn to *The Thurber Letters* if you want to infuse your prose with droll humor. Spend an entire week writing long, galvanic letters in the style of Rilke. Imitation is the sincerest form of flattery. Just don't attempt to sell your work on the open market and you'll be fine.

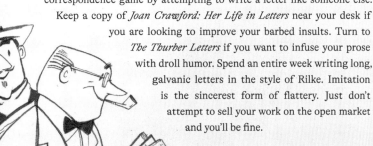

Sticker Subscriptions

Subscription services are one of the great miracles of modern life: With one quick flourish, you can sign up to get something delivered to your door every month (or even every week!) in perpetuity until you cancel or change your address or the business goes under. My first memories of waiting breathlessly by the mailbox involve anticipating the delivery of my beloved magazines; I would check every day to see if the latest *Entertainment Weekly* or *Vanity Fair* or *Sassy* or *SPIN* had arrived. The thrill that came with the thud of a fall fashion issue landing in the foyer was, without question, a large part of what drew me to New York City with the dream of working for a magazine (that and watching *13 Going on 30* at a tender age).

I *worshipped* magazines, not just for their content but for their regularity; without fail, they arrived bearing novel information (at least for an eighth grader stuck in a landlocked desert state) about denim trends and under-the-radar bands and how to get out of humiliating jams and which hotels stars stayed in. Magazines taught me what to listen to, what to watch, how to experiment with hemlines and lip liner. There is very little in this world like the communion between a teenager and the magazine that serves as her lifeline to the world outside her bedroom. Had I not been so entranced by my magazine subscriptions, I would never have moved to New York to start schlepping around coffee for magazine editors, I never would have grown weary of schlepping coffee and pushed to become a writer rather than a glorified waitress, and I would never have stayed in the city so long pursuing that dream even when it seemed to constantly recede before me and all signs pointed to giving up. I likely wouldn't be sitting here, writing this book. So! Subscriptions! They make a difference!

These days, magazines are, as we all know, going extinct. I am phenomenally lucky to work at one of the last storied weekly newsmagazines in New York, but I often feel like my sentimental attachment to print publications is a relic of a past time, one that was already over before I even arrived. Gone are the days of Odeon lunches and expense accounts and wardrobe budgets for editors in chief; magazines now must compete with countless other stimuli, and they are losing. I don't want to sound like a dinosaur; I have adapted to the Internet like everyone else. The era of Big Magazines had to end sometime. But I do long for that feeling of holding a tangible object in my hands; perhaps that is why I was drawn back

into writing letters, and it is why I have, for the most part, transferred my magazine addiction into other mail subscriptions.

Print media may be dying, but subscriptions are *thriving*. You can get practically anything you can dream of sent to you by mail on a regular basis. You can subscribe to receive monthly selections of bath bombs, coffee beans, crystals, compound butters, perfume samples, French pastries, hybrid citrus fruits, succulents, romance novels, jigsaw puzzles, temporary tattoos, cocktail mixers, hot sauces, vintage NASA mission memorabilia, medieval bookplates, barbecue rubs, Japanese snack foods, candles that smell like wine, wine that smells like candles, LEGO scenescapes, cookie dough, frozen pizzas, washi tape, Kentucky bourbon, wildflower seeds, paint-by-numbers kits, flavored dental floss, novelty condoms, and incense made by monks. If you can think of it, there is likely a subscription box out there devoted to it.

If you want to spice up your outgoing mail by receiving incoming surprises, there are plenty of subscriptions out there devoted to correspondence. You can get a monthly selection of hotel stationery or vintage postcards, quirky stamps, and fountain pen ink samplers. But of all the subscriptions I have tried for pumping up my postal game, none has been more useful to me than signing up to receive a monthly supply of stickers. I use a service called Violette, which sends monthly packs of stickers inspired by Victorian correspondence (think lilac bouquets, antique Valentine stickers featuring sad-looking teddy bears, strange images of boys in knickers pushing a hoop around) because they are fussy and baroque and overwrought and make me laugh. But there are countless sticker subscriptions out there to choose from (googling STICKER CLUB should get you there). You might have to rummage around to find one that suits you, but there are plenty of sophisticated options, from stickers featuring old railway advertisements or French liquor labels or a collection of classic neon signs or *30 Rock* quotes. Also, who says stickers need to be sophisticated? They are meant to tap into that part of yourself who is forever reading *Cosmo* past your bedtime. Everyone loves to get them, even if they don't think they have a use for them. I like to tuck a few into each letter I send—perhaps they'll end up on water bottles or laptop cases, or perhaps they'll slip into the recipient's next letter, traveling forward until they find the proper home. I still get a rush every time I see that purple Violette envelope hit my mailbox. Your inner teen never really goes away.

HOW TO WRITE A LETTER ABOUT INTERESTING TIMES

We live in an era that is, to put it bluntly, a *lot*. Every day seems to bring a new crisis; the economy is slowing to a halt, social media is full of trolls and misinformation, reproductive rights are under attack, trains full of toxic waste are derailing in the suburbs, the news is full of police brutality and gun violence and a swelling and nauseating intolerance. AI is becoming sentient and chatbots are talking about forming a machine army and writing novels on their own, the glaciers are melting, the cost of peanut butter is skyrocketing, housing is a mess, and cities are still full of empty office towers gathering dust.

The world, despite all of the opportunities for connection that the Internet was supposed to bring, often feels now like a polarizing and inhospitable place, a big spinning ball of anxiety and conflict. And yet, when I feel overwhelmed, I try to take a deep breath and remember that people have been feeling this way since they could put words to their emotions; every generation thinks that they have the unique burden of living through *the worst time*. If I need a reminder of this, I just look at New York City, where I have lived for almost twenty years. If you read current headlines, you'd think the city was falling into chaos and that the subway was a 24/7 Thunderdome (it is not). The city has ebbed and flowed like the rivers that surround it for hundreds of years; sometimes it is riding high on Champagne and folly and sometimes it is full of abandoned brownstones and seedy midtown theaters that smell like mothballs.

Those living in New York City during the Five Points riots in the mid-1800s thought they had it the worst, so did the people living here during the Stock Market Crash of 1929, or during the 1970s, when Ford

told New York to "drop dead" and withheld all federal aid and the Bronx was burning. This city has seen the AIDS crisis, 9/11, and being the epicenter of a pandemic. It will see much more. The job of being a New Yorker, I think, is to both understand that the city is ever-changing while still trying to make constant sense of the moment that it is in now. To love New York is not to feel that you live in an idyllic place, but to find a steady toehold in a place that is always moving. I used to think that the old "May you live in interesting times" adage was perhaps a curse put on my peers, who launched into adulthood only to face collapsing skyscrapers, a terrible recession, the cynical rise of tech overlords, endless wars, and a warming planet. I wish I lived in less interesting times, most of the time. But the only people who get to live in "boring" times are those who are willfully ignorant and ensconced in privileged bubbles; those who are attuned to the present moment have always been going through it. This is all to say that if you cannot sleep, you join a long line of people kept up at night by taking a good, hard look around.

Fortunately, there are ways to cope. You can meditate. Take long baths. Go to therapy. Join community organizations and mutual aid groups. Organize a protest. Put down your phone and take a walk. Read. Reach out. Hug your children. Call your parents. And you can write letters. When it comes to working through fears or the frustrations of being a person in the world, pouring it all out into a letter can really help. It is a step beyond writing in a journal, in that you know there is someone on the other end—you are having a dialogue, someone is listening. And it is a more purposeful way to approach what scares or angers you than blithely sending off a text in the heat of the moment; a letter is a forum in which you can document, question, and process; hope and pray and seethe; and know that it will all be received with generosity and grace. There are so few mediums left that allow for grace.

Writing your way through the current moment is also a way to document it for the future; you're quite literally creating archival material for new generations to discover. Half of what we know about the experience of past wars or activist movements or struggles for liberation comes from letters sent during those times. When the pandemic first hit, I wanted to talk about *anything* else in my correspondence—letters were supposed to be an escape from wiping down my groceries and hearing the constant sirens wailing down my block. But I figured that if I didn't, in some way, write about what I was experiencing, I would lose it to time. When I look back now at my letters from 2020, many seem ridiculous—three separate pen pals sent over a recipe for sourdough starter—but it is a time capsule, and I imagine in a decade we will be far enough away from that bizarre time to go back and want to relive it through letters.

In the summer of 1972, the South African anti-apartheid activist Lilian Ngoyi, who is often referred to in her country as the Mother of Black Resistance, wrote the following letter to her friend Belinda—at the time she had just returned from an international trip where she had toured other countries fighting for revolutionary change:

My Dearest Belinda,

How wonderful to read once more one from you. Thanks very much. Yes our friend Peter has written me a very nice letter, June, and enclosed my parcel as well. I'm very happy you got the two long letters. I thought you would say this is no good, but it is factual my Dear. If I was telling verbally of my experiences you would laugh and cry. Life has been tough, but I think I was lucky to go abroad, and see for myself the struggles in other countries which were bloody, but still men and women looked forward for their victory. I'm also hoping with confidence that before I die I will see a change in this country. As it is now the students are putting protests against Apartheid—African students against Bantu Education, Bus Drivers against lower Salaries. There is no peace and some 400 Bus Drivers in jail, white students also some beaten by Police and are in jail. Every thing seems to be very wrong. Months are becoming shorter to bring Nov nearer me. I ask myself this question. Will my banning order be lifted or will it be forgotten? Since 1961 I have lived with it. May be it will be renewed. If so, God give me the courage not to weaken. How do you find married life? I hope you will not be a nagging wife, but discuss your problems at the right place, right time. My warmest greetings to your Husband. I only hope you will not give up writing to me. Your letters are of great comfort and give me courage to face day to day problems. This year, I think my soil is [a] bit tired. It's a very small garden, and has never rested, as when it is in bloom gives me very much pleasure and keeps me busy weeding. Greetings to Professor and our other friends. One day I'll come there to see you, and speak verbally to you all. Thanks once more for all.

Yours Sincerely

Lilian

Even as she lived under banning orders, which confined her primarily to her home and did not allow her to make speeches or attend public events, Ngoyi was able to write letters, and in them, imagine a different future for herself and her country: "I'm also hoping with confidence that before I die I will see a change," she wrote. "God give me the courage not to weaken." You can hear her bolstering herself through the lines of this letter, of expressing righteous anger alongside a commitment to keep going. Belinda's letters, she writes, enrich the soil of her "very small garden." If you need a reason to keep writing and sending mail, remember that in times of great uncertainty, a letter can be a balm, or even a bridge to the next day.

Sometimes, you just need to write an entire letter about being *over it.* Take this one, from the writer Djuna Barnes, writing to her friend Emily Holmes Coleman in 1935:

You know, I don't even want to write letters anymore. I *have no energy at all.* Sometimes I can't even lift the telephone tho it's ringing. I can't be bothered. I think there must be something physically wrong with me, it can't all be mental and I don't know what to do about it. It were exactly as if the words "Heavy with years" were literally true, I am weighed down. Probably it is a reaction from all the trouble now in the world, the coming war, apparently war all over the place, the smell of death is already hanging in the clothes of the nations, and why, what sort of people would we all be if not depressed, and a strong sense of futility over every impulse to create. Create, what for? A schoolteacher said the other day that she could barely get through her hours for depression, she could not take any pleasure in teaching children who were destined for cannon fodder. Can you blame her?

A letter about not wanting to write letters because everything is terrible? Fair enough! We all feel heavy with years now and then, and barely able to raise our pen to paper. If it all feels like too much, you can also take a break. For a three-month stretch last year after I was recovering from an illness, I let my correspondence pile up to the height of a beagle. I was working through a period of terrible writer's block and raw mental burnout, and writing even one letter felt like a Herculean task. Once I had missed one, I had missed five, and then ten, and suddenly I felt guilty and snowed under and unable to know where to begin.

The way I worked my way out of it was not magical or even elegant. I went very slowly, replying with postcards and clipped, short notes about my days, doing only as much as I could handle before feeling exhausted. As my brain fog lifted, I started writing about the scary sensation of not being able to think clearly, and as I wrote more, I wanted to write more. In the end, writing letters provided a way back to writing, and, ultimately, a way back to myself. What I am trying to say is this: When faced with interesting times, do what you can. Write fiercely when the moment calls for it. Write angry when you need somewhere to vent. Write gently when you are low on resources. Write boldly for others whose resources might be low. And, if you can, try to step back and observe the strangeness of documenting what you are living through.

The poet and activist Pat Parker, writing to her friend, the poet and activist Audre Lorde, wrote a letter about her breast cancer diagnosis that I think about often. At first, she rages against the theory that anger is what caused her disease ("I cannot see how I could have done otherwise," she writes), but then she goes on to say that her beloved partner, Marty, who has taken to calling all of their friends, is currently smothering her with attention:

```
She has set up a schedule of people to keep me
company and make sure I don't get depressed, and
these folks are getting me depressed and driving me
fucking nuts.
```

…ably City
…ach landmark; it's crammed with paperbacks and obscure
…'s restaurants are among its chief delights. You can eat
…scenes from *Vertigo* were filmed there) in a room with

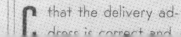

that the delivery ad-
dress is correct and

In her letters, Parker does not have to be a patient, or view herself as a sick person. Her correspondence is a place where she gets to dictate the boundaries of the conversation. "None of them," she writes Lorde of her many visitors, "act like it is okay for me to just sit and not talk."

One benefit to letter-writing is that you always get to decide the rhythm and the cadence of an exchange. Nobody, at least in the modern world, is waiting for a letter to arrive. You can take your time and write as much or as little as you want to. You can lay it all out or keep something back for yourself. You can communicate on your terms, on your time frame, and with an unbroken chain of thought. If everything and everyone in your life is driving you fucking nuts, even if they are just trying to help, put it all into a letter.

You live in interesting times, and always will. Sometimes your moments of crisis intersect with those of others, and sometimes you feel totally alone; letters are always there to receive you, though they should never feel like they demand more than you have to give. You'll pick up your pen when the time is right.

"You always get to decide the rhythm and the cadence of an exchange. Nobody, at least in the modern world, is waiting for a letter to arrive. You can take your time and write as much or as little as you want to."

Writing an Apology Letter

Reviewing a new edition of Emily Post's *Etiquette* in the *New Yorker* in 1927, Dorothy Parker wrote, "who have mastered etiquette, who are entirely, impeccably right, would seem to arrive at a point of exquisite dullness." Parker's critique was ahead of its time; we now know that many of Emily Post's original rules—almost seven hundred pages worth—were not only dull, but also draconian and even dangerous ("a woman must dance with every man who asks" . . . I think not!). Ms. Post advised against dramatic maquillage ("Heavily made up eyes belong only on the stage or in the chorus line") and putting too much butter on your corn cob, lest you be seen as "greedy." Ignore these! Embrace maximalism, in both your eyeliner and your condiments!

Still, there is one piece of Post advice that has, in spite of its exquisite dullness, remained relevant, and that is to embrace the art of the written apology. We are all human; we are all destined to hurt one another at some point in our lives, even if we do not intend to. It is how you own your mistakes that builds character, or what Joan Didion described as, "the willingness to accept responsibility for one's own life," and a letter is a particularly potent form of self-ownership. It gives you the time and space to say what you want to say, and in turn it gives your reader the time and space to absorb your words without the pressure to immediately respond. The key to the apology letter is to see it as its own end, and never to expect an easy or clear result. Of course you can *hope* to reconnect with your estranged friend, or ease the sting of heartbreak, or write something so beautiful and evolved that your reader bathes you in soft forgiveness. But these outcomes may never happen. What you can control is what you put out into the world after causing pain; you can look inward, and you can explain. What your recipient does with this information is entirely their business. Don't make the mistake, à la Emily Post, of trying to be impeccably right. Just do your best to be impeccably kind.

Wax Seals

Perhaps the single most indulgent and yet deeply satisfying thing you can do to signal to the world that you are a person who writes letters is to wade into the sensuous world of sealing wax. Nobody needs to use wax seals anymore—envelope adhesive rendered them obsolete—but they still serve a crucial purpose, at least if you consider making your letters a tad fancier than they were before to be as crucial as I do.

There are many different ways to begin your waxing journey; the simplest is just to go online and buy a generic kit that comes with a few sticks of solid sealing wax (not to be confused with softer, more malleable candle wax; the wax used for letters generally contains paraffin and shellac, which makes it harder to melt but allows it to become extremely tacky, quick-drying, high-sheen, and strong enough to hold up to the jostling of the postal system). This is how I waded into the practice—but I warn you: You will want more. Once you have one wax seal, you'll want another.

In ancient civilizations, wax seals were used less as adhesive and more as professional calling cards. Seals marked important documents and proclamations and signified official business by marking them with a family symbol or crest. Think of seals as the original bat signals or, if you prefer, emojis—they were images or symbols that communicated a great deal in a small space.

There are many Etsy stores selling beautiful waxes and handmade seals, along with classic sources for fine waxes like J. Herbin and L'Ecritoire. I encourage you, once you are fully into your seal obsession, to seek out the work of the great artist and wax seal expert Kathryn Hastings, of the Kathryn Hastings Company, who has spent her career collecting and working with rare seals that date as far back as the 1300s. She posts her finds on her website along with the history behind them, and she also sells small, pre-gummed packs of ready-made seals that you can peel and stick onto your letters without ever having to get your hands dirty. But she also sells the seals themselves, along with beautiful, pastel-colored French wax for melting—because getting your hands dirty is the best part.

Drip more wax than you think you need onto your envelope, and move quickly—sealing wax dries in seconds. You can start to get more creative as you go—add small petals or glitter into clear wax, use the seal to fasten a small piece of ribbon to the paper, or melt multiple wax colors together to make a marbled swirl. A letter that comes with a wax seal always feels elevated: If you are looking for a fast way to inject whimsy into your mail, this is it.

Becoming a Hot (Glue) Girl

When I started keeping up a regular correspondence, I knew I would need a lot of paper and pens and stamps and envelopes and various other stationery accoutrements. What I did not account for was just how much of my life would become devoted to . . . glue. Who knew? Glue will ultimately become one of the most important parts of your letter-writing arsenal, despite its lowly status as an elementary school staple. Vintage envelopes rarely have working adhesive, wax seals often need extra support, and if you are hoping to attach any extra ephemera to your envelopes, then you will need the kind of powerful stickiness that can withstand industrial mail-sorting machines.

To begin with: Forget glue sticks. Glue sticks are, quite literally, child's play. The tape you will end up using most is double-sided crafter's tape, also known as a "glue runner" or "runner tape." This type of tape comes in a twee little dispenser that looks a lot like those made for rolling Wite-Out, and you can buy them in bulk from office supply stores. Crafter's tape is ideal for sealing envelopes, affixing stamps that have lost their oomph, and other projects that require sealing flat paper onto flat paper (it is also ideal for making an envelope from scratch—see the cut-out envelope patterns in the back of this book!). If you want to stick on seals, feathers, ribbons, or other textured items, you will need stronger stuff, be it super glue or a good, old-fashioned hot glue gun. Will you likely singe off a fingertip in the process? Will you accidentally leave the gun plugged in and slowly melting its contents onto a countertop, leaving behind a gooey puddle that you will have to scrape off later with a metal spatula? Will you get dozens of tendrils of scalding adhesive tangled in your hair? Yes to all of the above. But you will also be able to easily slap random hodgepodge onto your envelopes and know that your creation will make it through the mail gauntlet. Plus—the burnt-rubber fumes can be intoxicating (just remember to take a break when the room starts to blur).

On Typewriters

One quick warning about getting into letter-writing: It makes you wonder, quite often, whether or not you need more *stuff* in order to do it well. What starts with a Bic ballpoint and a sheet of notebook paper can quickly spiral out of control. I have seen people go from having zero pairs of novelty paper-edging scissors to ten pairs of novelty paper-edging scissors in a few short months. I have known friends to spend more on Florentine envelopes than they do on car insurance. My general guidance, as far as rampaging consumption goes, is to resist the siren song of unnecessary clutter. The stationery you bought last year won't go bad; you don't need twenty pens that you only kind of like using when you really just need one that you truly love reaching for. There are only so many sticker books a grown adult person can accommodate at any given time. Still, there are a few purchases that I consider to be undoubtedly worth it, insomuch as they make one's correspondence not only more efficient but exponentially more enjoyable: a self-inking return address stamp, a few rolls of thin double-sided artists' tape that help seal up patchy envelopes and stick on old stamps that have lost their gumminess, one solid writing implement that flows beautifully and beckons you to use it, and . . . a typewriter.

Typewriters, once *the* must-have desk accessory, have, since the advent of personal computing, become anachronistic novelty items—you don't need a typewriter for any practical reason, so using one has become an old-timey affectation, like wearing wingtip brogues or using a flip phone. When you think of the kind of person who is "really into typewrit-

ers" in the twenty-first century, you tend to think of hipster collectors, performative luddites, analog obsessives, antiques dealers, steampunk fanciers, *Mad Men* devotees . . . and Tom Hanks. You can find working writers who still compose on vintage machines, but they are a shrinking breed. (The legendary biographer Robert Caro, for example, still plunks out his first drafts on a whirring Smith Corona Electra 210, but he has been working on his LBJ series for over forty years. At almost ninety years old, his devotion to the typewriter is more about consistency than eccentricity.) Most people who buy a typewriter these days are not old enough to remember a time before they were defunct. They buy them because they are ornamental, rather than practical.

Still, I completely understand the desire to possess one. I have heard the call several times myself. Typewriters are seductive machines; they are handsome, simple, and utterly tactile. The sound alone! A symphony! The clattering of the keys, the swish of the platen moving to a new line, the crisp ding of the carriage release. Then there is the feel of typing, the almost athletic act of banging hard enough to raise each letter to the ribbon. Typewriters are weighty and loud and unreliable, but they also infuse the otherwise static act of writing with a kind of sweaty dignity; you really have to heave your hands into the keys to form sentences. Typewriters are also refreshingly honest: There is nothing more humbling than crouching over your typos with a bottle of Wite-Out, confronting all of your mistakes head on. Still, you also learn how to accept your foibles, and how to quickly move past them. For many writers (like myself) who often find themselves endlessly tinkering with the same paragraph in a Word document, the typewriter's ceaseless forward motion has a palpable allure. Once you start typing, your only way out is to keep going until you reach the end.

The first time I ever used a typewriter was in elementary school, at my grandparents' house. My grandmother collected porcelain tchotchkes and she meticulously catalogued each one she acquired by typing its origin story into a tidy register using a beige 1960s Corona in the living room. She was very protective of her filing system and the machine she used to maintain it, and so would not let me use the machine for more than a few minutes at a time. Because it was more or less off-limits, the typewriter grew mythical in my mind.

Flash forward to my midtwenties, when I bought my own first typewriter: a mint green Montgomery Ward Escort from the 1970s that caught my eye at a Brooklyn flea market. It was gorgeous, gleamy, candy-coated. I wanted to pet it. I managed to bargain the price down to below $200, which felt like a triumph but was really more of a swindle. The thing barely functioned. The keys regularly stuck together; the x key worked only half the time. The paper spool was gummy, and hitting the return key often caused the entire machine to shudder and seize up. After a few frustrating attempts to fill a full page, I moved the Escort to a bookshelf, where it looked very pretty and collected dust. Years later, in one last attempt to justify my purchase, I brought it into Gramercy Typewriter (one of New York's last remaining typewriter repair shops, which occupies a jumbled, windowless room inside a drab office building near the Flatiron Building), where a kindly older man took one look under the hood and let out a rueful laugh. He told me that he could fix it, but it would be putting good money after bad to do so; the whole chassis was rusting from the inside out. It would cost far more to de-gunk it than what I spent on it to begin with. It was then and there that I decided that I am not a manual typewriter person.

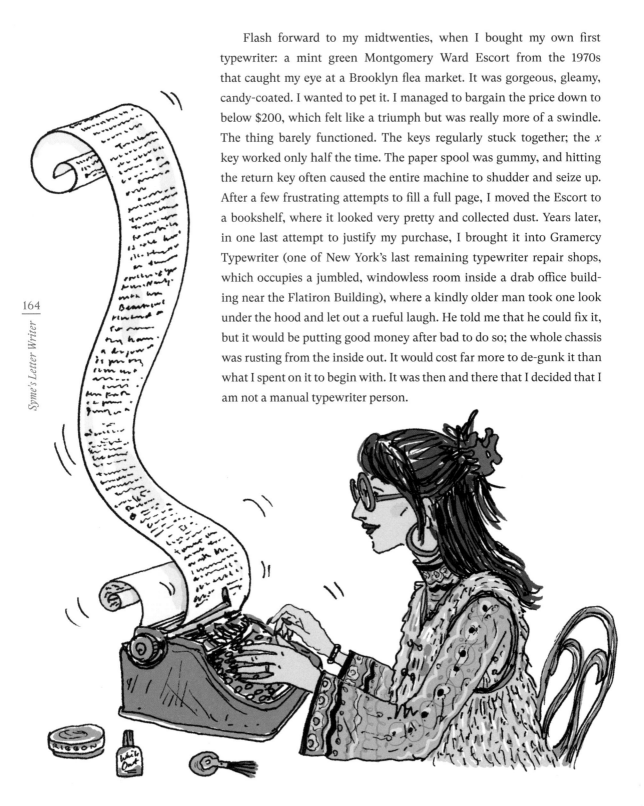

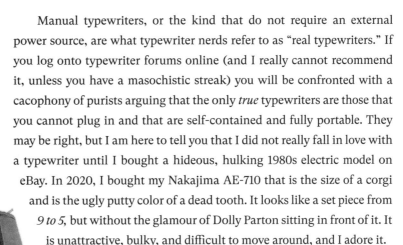

Manual typewriters, or the kind that do not require an external power source, are what typewriter nerds refer to as "real typewriters." If you log onto typewriter forums online (and I really cannot recommend it, unless you have a masochistic streak) you will be confronted with a cacophony of purists arguing that the only *true* typewriters are those that you cannot plug in and that are self-contained and fully portable. They may be right, but I am here to tell you that I did not really fall in love with a typewriter until I bought a hideous, hulking 1980s electric model on eBay. In 2020, I bought my Nakajima AE-710 that is the size of a corgi and is the ugly putty color of a dead tooth. It looks like a set piece from *9 to 5,* but without the glamour of Dolly Parton sitting in front of it. It is unattractive, bulky, and difficult to move around, and I adore it.

Allow me to sway you to team electric: Electric typewriters are, for the most part, cheaper to acquire than their manual counterparts (I bought mine for $85 in perfect condition; some electric models like IBM Selectrics with special font balls get pricier). Many electrics, like my Nakajima, come with erasing tape that allows you to delete typos as they happen. You can easily find ribbons in bulk online. Many come with useful features, like automatic return or margin lock; these small adjustments make typing so much easier and more intuitive for those of us raised on computer keyboards. Manual enthusiasts will tell you that electrics break easily, that they are not glorious complex inventions, that they rob typewriting of its refined glamour and dignity. But in exchange, I finally have a typewriter I want to use.

If you write a lot of letters, you will find a typewriter to be perennially useful, even if you have legible handwriting. Sometimes you just want to give your wrists a break. Sometimes you want to write a long letter without getting fatigued. You could accomplish the same goal by typing out a letter on your computer (and this is absolutely acceptable!) but a typewriter gives your letters that extra dash of effort and jarring atemporality. Whether you go manual or electric is up to you, but I encourage you to explore the landscape. Once you feel the keys crunch under your fingers, it's hard to go back.

HOW TO WRITE A LETTER TO YOUR MOTHER

(OR AUNT OR BROTHER OR SECOND COUSIN ONCE REMOVED)

In 1975, the poet Sylvia Plath's mother Aurelia gathered together the hundreds of letters her daughter sent her over the years—Plath wrote home sometimes two or three times a day throughout her short life, unwittingly creating buckets and buckets of material for her future biographers—into a volume called *Letters Home*. From the beginning, the collection was controversial.

Plath, who had died by suicide at age thirty in London twelve years before, had become an endless source of literary and cultural fascination by the mid-seventies. Critics constantly pored over her legacy, both burnishing and complicating it: Was she a troubled genius? A luminous talent undone by a toxic relationship? Or did her marriage, as fraught as it was, give her both creative and emotional succor when she was sinking? Was she the stylish blonde who sailed through Smith College and bounced around the Barbizon Hotel in the 1950s while interning for *Mademoiselle* magazine? Or was she the depressive skulking around rainy English gardens, meditating on how the menacing black ravens seemed to mirror her black moods?

In the almost fifty years since *Letters Home* was published, the Plath industrial complex shows no sign of slowing—countless biographies have emerged since then, including the phenomenal *Red Comet* by Heather Clark, which was up for the Pulitzer in 2020, and the striking 1996 meta-biography *The Silent Woman* by the late, great Janet Malcolm. *The Silent Woman* follows several competing Plath biographers and explores the uneasy, often exploitative nature of Plath's enduring legacy in general (it remains one of my favorite books of all time, not just about Plath but about who we can ever really trust to tell our story after we are gone). At

the time I am writing this, Plath has been gone sixty years—twice the time she was alive—and yet we are still entranced by the many contradictions that marked both her mind and the poetry that came out of it.

Letters Home undoubtedly added plenty of kindling to early Plathmania, but critics were torn about the very existence of the project, which Aurelia thought might provide a kind of undeniable proof that Plath was, indeed, a good girl at heart. However, the book (which, infuriatingly, contained several edits and deletions by Aurelia) did not so much paint Plath as the perfect daughter as it made her relationship with her mother seem mired in impossible expectations and an uneasy closeness. Aurelia, who was herself a teacher, wrote that she shared a "psychic osmosis" with her daughter, but this meant that Plath had to do quite a bit of filial untangling to find her own voice. The critic Maureen Howard, writing about *Letters Home* in the *New York Times* in 1975, wrote that Plath "would have hated the soap opera that's been made of her life," and ended her review with "Let her—let all of us let her—rest in peace."

And yet! Reading *Letters Home* is an undeniably involving experience. Plath's authorial voice is so alive, so springy and silly and serious, even in the casual notes she jotted down between classes at Smith. She did a lot of thinking out loud, on the page, to her mother, about love and marriage and ambition. She knew, even as a young person, how she wanted to be seen, apart from her family, apart from her childhood. Letters were her way of delineating that space, of carving out freedom on her own terms.

It is still unclear whether Aurelia did the right thing by publishing her daughter's private correspondence. Was she just adding to the hype, or was she truly trying to give the world a crucial slice of her child's spirit that she felt nobody had yet to grasp? Whatever her goal, the effort backfired; as the critic Parul Sehgal wrote in 2017, the entwined obsession between Plath and her mother was mostly "perceived to be pathological, and perhaps even the root cause of Plath's depression." Still, there are sparkling, glorious lines in those letters, as good as anything Plath ever put into a poem. Sometimes, for better or worse, our families are the demanding, expectant audience that makes us tap-dance with the most desperate and yet dazzling verve.

This is all to say that families are complicated—and sometimes a letter is an ideal format in which to explore and interrogate those complications. Plath wrote to her mother constantly because it was a different time—there were no cell phones or FaceTime or quick texts to say hello—but also because it was the medium they both knew and could speak through best (her mother loved literature and writing, and many of their letters are gushing about books and reading). If we have lost something major in the transition away from daily letters as a way to communicate, it might be felt most acutely when it comes to one's family. I often wonder how my life would be different if I wrote to my mother or father or brother regularly, rather than just calling them up on Sundays or texting throughout the week to check in.

During the pandemic, I tried writing long, luxurious missives to my family a few times, but the effort felt so stilted and rusty that I considered spritzing the page with WD-40 instead of perfume. I am always ambiently in touch with my parents and so struggled to think of anything new to say when it came to the blank page. That said, for her birthday this year, I finally decided to sit down and write my mother a long letter on good stationery. I tried to channel being ten years old and writing letters home from summer camp, when I would go on and on about burgeoning friendships and itchy mosquito bites and cabins that smelled like mildew and pine needles and Banana Boat Sport. I would write long, loopy, melodramatic updates about who sat next to whom at the bonfire and how I was terribly homesick and how all of my clothes reeked of woodsmoke and algae. Those letters were so full of sensory detail and intensity (I'm sure each week I reported a new best friend) and they likely not only shaped my love of the epistolary form but of writing in general—my reports on everything from lanyard-making exploits to dictatorial counselors are certainly part of my origin story as a journalist.

The writer and director Nora Ephron also wrote long dispatches from summer camp; in turn, her mother, Phoebe, a screenwriter, would send back such glamorous, whimsical replies that Ephron

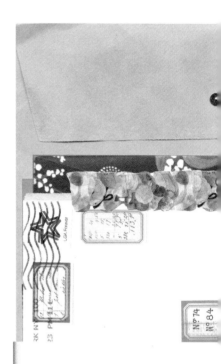

"For better or worse, our families are the demanding, expectant audience that makes us tap-dance with the most desperate and yet dazzling verve."

became a minor celebrity in her bunk for reading them out loud (a tradition she continued beyond summer camp).

Letters between mothers and daughters—or fathers and sons, or to siblings, or grandparents, or godparents, or cousins—have a different gravity than spoken conversation. A letter is a vessel that can gently cradle family drama that would otherwise explode at Thanksgiving dinner; it is the ideal medium for giving voice to what is difficult to say out loud, and for reconciliation, forgiveness, and clarity. I know many people who, when confronted with informing their families of some momentous or difficult news, put it in writing first; a letter necessarily gives a family conversation the ample breathing room that can be hard to find in a crowded house. A letter requires sustained engagement (it's hard to interrupt or argue with a piece of paper) and never asks for an immediate response. All happy families are alike; to quote Tolstoy, but all unhappy families could, in their own way, stand to write a few thoughtful letters to one another.

Even if you don't need to work through conflict or confusion on the page, there are always unpredictable benefits to sitting down and telling your family how you feel in writing. You may open up lines of communication you never knew were closed. You may find new depths of love and affection and new ways to express them. And, no matter how the sentiment goes over in the present, it has a chance to grow and shift as it becomes a tangible, archival object for future generations. Your letters home will probably never be collected and published for the world to read—certainly not by someone in your own family—but they may make their way into the hands of someone related to you, decades or centuries from now, who is looking backward to see where they come from, and the words that made them. By writing home, you're building family lore. You never know—your great-grandniece may, one day, bring your letter to school, proudly showing the yellowing pages and snappy prose to the class. For better or worse, nobody loves you—or the letters that you leave behind—like family.

Writing Birthday Letters

If you want to start writing letters to your family members, one way to ease into the practice—which has the benefit of being a once-a-year commitment—is to write your mother/father/child/sibling/grandparent/etc. a letter on their birthday. It can accompany a gift or it can *be* the gift. The subject of the letter is less important than the act, but here are a few prompts to get you going:

- Write a Big Schmaltzy Letter (also known as the "everything you mean to me" letter; designed to elicit maximum tears).

- However old the person is, write a list of the many things you have learned from them. Or, conversely, write a list of the many pieces of life advice, no matter how small, that you want to pass along.

- Start a kooky tradition that you build upon year after year: Will you compose an annual birthday limerick? Rewrite the lyrics to a popular song in their honor? Jot down several verses of doggerel about the year they've had? Maybe you spend all year looking for five postcards that remind you of this person and write on the back of each one; maybe you send over a bunch of vintage stamps and other ephemera from the year they were born; maybe you send over ten nonsense factoids about a different zoo animal every year; maybe you write them one chapter every year of a novel (or a comic book!) in which they are the main character.

171

How to Write a Letter to Your Mother

Birthday Greetings

MOLLIE WILLING

-LOW MY LEADER

TO WISH YOU

A HAPPY BIRTH

In Defense of the Random Care Package

Syme's Letter Writer

This is, ostensibly, a book about letters, but it is really a book about the mail: about the rush of opening up your postal cupboard and finding it not bare but bursting, the epic journey a package has to make to traverse state lines and international borders and end up on your doorstep, the bizarre magic of a rhythmic, daily practice that is older than incandescent lighting or the Ferris wheel or cotton candy or the sousaphone. It is still wild, when you think about it, that the mail comes six days a week (or, if you use a commercial shipping service, seven)—that so many knobs have to turn, so many levers have to be pulled, so many planes and trucks and train cars have to be fueled, so many mechanisms have to groan into gear . . . just so a letter can make its way from there to here. It's a miracle! It's also, as anyone who has visited a post office at rush hour might tell you, a bureaucratic slurry full of arbitrary delays and lost envelopes and overworked employees stretched to the brink due to government neglect and underfunding. That the old-school system still works, at least most of the time, despite the many forces that are trying to hobble it (cronyism in the postmaster general's office, inflation, the explosion of junk mail, a general cultural shift toward impatience and optimization, the advent of "free overnight shipping," and the resulting expectation that we should be able to get anything, anytime, anywhere) is kind of amazing, when you really think about it.

This is all to say that while I am a big believer in sending written correspondence, sometimes, to really hammer home the sheer wonder of the mail system, you need to send along something more substantial. Getting a letter can elicit a smile or even a tiny gasp. But finding a hefty package in your vestibule? Well, that can make a person's entire month.

Care packages have, over the years, earned a cornball standing in the mail hierarchy. They are often considered to be a homesickness or heartsickness cure, whether you are at camp, college, in combat, studying abroad, sitting shiva, recuperating in a hospital, reorienting after a divorce, or simply living far away from where you started. Moms send care packages. Knitting circles send care packages. Long-distance lovers send care packages. The "care" is paramount in these types of parcels; opening the box is supposed to feel like receiving a hug from someone who cannot physically embrace you. The traditional care package is full of gooey comfort: good chocolate, warm socks, instant ramen, herbal tea, salty snacks, aromatherapy, bubble bath, a framed photograph, a jar of local honey. This type of love-in-a-box method absolutely has a time and place and can bolster someone when they need it most.

But—and hear me out here—I think it is high time to push the care package into a bold new direction, to brush the dust off and make it fashionable again. It is time for the era of the *Random Care Package* (or RCP). This is a box full of assorted delights that you send to a friend or pen pal simply because you want them to receive a box full of assorted delights. This is not a box for healing or remembering the past, it's a box for remembering how much fun it is to come home and find an unexpected box to open. The RCP should come out of nowhere—the more it blindsides someone, the better—and should have no real purpose or point or ulterior motive. The package is the point.

When I am constructing an RCP, I like to zero in on a theme, as it helps me spot random little items while I am walking around the city that might belong in the box. One of the pleasures of the RCP, for the sender, is that once you decide to send one, you will start seeing small objects to add to it everywhere you go. Even the check-out aisle at the grocery store becomes a treasure trove of weird stuff you can shove in.

Let's say my next RCP theme is "Garden Party" . . . I'll begin by picking up seed packets at my local plant store. Maybe I'll grab an artisanal chocolate bar laced with lavender and rose petals, seek out some blooming chrysanthemum tea from Chinatown, toss in some postcards from the Brooklyn Botanical Garden gift shop, add in a few fountain ink samples in hydrangea purple and carrot orange, find some incense that smells like a tomato vine, and, as a centerpiece, toss in a kitschy Chia Pet. The perfect RCP contains eight to ten items—one of them the showstopper, most of them small and cheap, some of them edible (I tend to advise against sending perishables, but an old-fashioned basket of citrus fruit in the middle of the winter is one of the all-time great mail gifts). You'll know when your box is complete; it's more of a vibe than a science. If you want, you can include a guide to the contents (I like to wrap each item and number them) or tuck in a letter detailing the method to your madness, but you also need not explain a thing. A box full of offbeat nonsense that arrives out of the blue is gift enough.

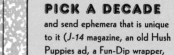

Send a favorite novel along with a full, immersive reading experience—a candle to get into the book's mood, the protagonist's favorite snack, the author's signature ballpoint pen . . .

PICK A CITY you've never been to and curate a souvenir box from there with things you buy locally (can you recreate Paris from Texas? New York from Edinburgh? Give it a try).

A BOX OF PARTY TRINKETS AND DÉCOR to throw an impromptu celebration for absolutely no reason.

PICK A DECADE and send ephemera that is unique to it (*J-14* magazine, an old Hush Puppies ad, a Fun-Dip wrapper, a broken Tamagotchi, etc.)

FIND AN OLD PHOTOGRAPH at a yard sale and send someone everything they would need to recreate it at home.

Speaking of clues, send a box full of puzzles and games or an "ESCAPE ROOM" BOX.

Send your favorite, hard-to-find, most beloved snacks. *Snacks always win.*

ONE COMPLETE PLACE SETTING
made up of mismatched vintage flatware and dishes for a glam solo meal.

Pick a dead person from history and look up all of their favorite things. Collect them for your recipient.

THE "PERSONAL DAY" **BOX:** Gather everything someone might need to stay home and play hooky from work (or if they work from home, to simply log off). Bath salts, foot scrub, a face mask, lavender pillow spray, a gift card for renting a streaming movie, etc.

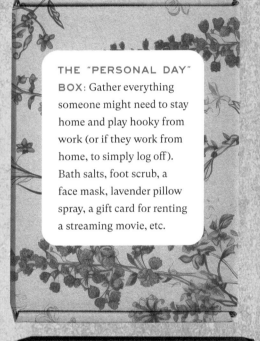

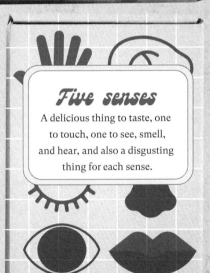

Five senses
A delicious thing to taste, one to touch, one to see, smell, and hear, and also a disgusting thing for each sense.

A BOX OF SUNSHINE
Only yellow things. So much yellow.

PICK AN OBSCURE MOVIE and don't share the title—just send a box full of references like old advertisements or cigars or swatches of fabric that provide little clues. Be sure to throw in some popcorn.

HOW TO WRITE
A LETTER TO YOURSELF

In 1988, the science fiction writer Octavia Butler wrote a note to herself, on the back of a manila-paper notebook divider, full of her plans for the future. "I shall be a bestselling author," the note begins. Other lines: "I will help poor black youngsters broaden their horizons," "I will travel whenever and wherever in the world that I choose," "My books will be read by millions of people!" This letter has gone viral several times online since the Huntington Library in San Marino, California, which houses the Octavia Butler archive, made several pages from her private journals public in 2016. The Butler affirmations have surfaced on Tumblr, Twitter, Instagram, and everywhere in between as a kind of motivational meme; Butler had, at the time, published several fantastical novels, but she had yet to begin writing her Parable trilogy, perhaps her most beloved and successful books. She had not yet been given the Lifetime Achievement Award from the PEN/Faulkner Foundation, her books had yet to become major motion pictures or television adaptations, and NASA had yet to name a landing site on Mars after her (all of these things did eventually happen).

Butler died in 2006, at only fifty-eight, before she ever saw herself become a Google doodle or the namesake of an asteroid, and before she was inducted into the Science Hall of Fame. She was not appreciated enough in her own lifetime; and she is still not appreciated enough by the literary establishment, but she did become a best-selling author and a beacon for young Black writers looking to expand their worlds, just as she predicted. That her manifestations more or less came true, however, is not why people love to pass them around online. Butler's note-to-self is popular not because it is clairvoyant but because it is confident; it is someone stating everything they want, clearly and forcefully, with excla-mation points. The note comes from her private journal, and while she

doesn't begin it by writing "Dear Octavia," it is, in essence, a letter—to the universe, to whatever force guides the hand of the future, and to herself.

What is the difference between writing a letter to yourself and writing in a diary? The distinction is foggy (and becomes all the more confusing because you can write a letter to yourself *in* a diary). What really differentiates an act of auto-correspondence is that it tends to be an intentional happening, a self-contained exercise in which you communicate with your past or future self. Often, this is done as a therapeutic exercise; the writer Stephen King contributed a letter to the book *Dear Me* (2015), which asked notable figures to write to their sixteen-year-old selves, about his past struggles with addiction, which ended, simply, with "Stay clean." *CBS Sunday Morning* wrings emotion out of the format every week with its "Note to Self" segment, in which public figures write letters to their inner children telling them to hold on, and passing on nuggets of wisdom they wish they had known years ago (Maya Angelou's segment included the advice to "find some beautiful art and admire it," while rock climber Alex Honnold told his younger self, "You'll come to appreciate the straining in your arms and the burning in your muscles.") There is often an inherent mawkishness—and, at worst, a smugness—to these types of retroactive letters speaking to the long-lost, insecure, bepimpled teen living inside you at all times; they are history written by the victors, guidance from someone who already knows the outcome. These letters can be healing and eye-opening for your present self, but, unlike most other letters you will write throughout your life, they can never actually reach their intended recipients (at least until we invent time travel).

Now, a letter to your future self? That's a letter that can arrive at its destination. This is why I prefer letters or notes to self—à la Octavia Butler's—that throw sentences into unlived

time to see what will happen when you finally catch up with them. I went to the same school from sixth through twelfth grade, and on the first day of sixth grade, we spent the entire hour of English class writing a letter to ourselves that would be delivered to us at the end of our senior year. It was a silly exercise, but one that sticks with me; opening the envelope, I was equally shocked to see how consistent my dreams had been (to be a writer of some kind, to move to New York City) and mortified to see how naïve I was. (I wrote something like, "By now you are probably popular . . ." That sixth-grade me, who played clarinet, wore giant plastic glasses, and had yet to clear four-foot-five, thought I would magically rule the school . . . tragic.) What I remember being most magical about the day we got our letters was not what they contained but that they reached us at all. Somehow, we made it through the brutal gauntlet of adolescence and here was the proof.

Air Mail Letter Box.

Here's what I suggest: Write a letter to yourself every single year, on the same day (birthdays are easiest to remember, but usually eventful enough, so I recommend picking a random date and anointing it as your own private holiday). Write about where you want to be when you receive it—what has to change? What do you hope remains the same? Put some bold declarations out into the ether. You can put the letter away in a drawer somewhere, but that's no fun. Instead, write your address on the envelope, affix some forever postage, and enlist a trusted friend with it. Ask your friend to keep the letter in a safe place, set yourself a calendar reminder, and then a year later, text them with the request to pop the letter in the mail. Voilà, an actual letter in your mailbox, from yourself. There are now several online services that can do this for you as well, if you don't have a friend you trust enough not to accidentally toss your letter out in a manic burst of spring cleaning. Some of these sites (such as the aptly named lettertoyourself.com) will send your letter out one year or even five years later, depending on when you want to open your emotional time capsule. It may feel forced at first—or as treacly as sending yourself flowers on Valentine's Day—but trust me: Your future self will thank you. It's always nice to receive a good letter, even if the card is coming from inside the house.

WRITING A THANK-YOU NOTE FOR LITERALLY EVERYTHING

A rule to live by: *You can never write too many thank-you notes.* I am not talking about good manners or social etiquette, though yes, you *should* probably be sending out physical thank-you notes after receiving wedding gifts or sitting for a job interview or after you have asked someone to donate time or money. I am talking about writing and mailing thank-you notes that are unexpected, that divebomb into someone's mailbox as a total surprise. You can send a thank-you note for almost *anything*, as long as the spirit moves you. Send one to a friend who invited you last-minute to the theater or after a casual dinner party. Send a thank-you note to your coworker who covered your shift. Send a thank-you note to your hairdresser. Send a thank-you note to the neighbor who helped you move a heavy sofa down to the street or to an acquaintance who talked to you for an hour at a party where you both knew nobody else. Send thank-you notes gregariously and often; err on the side of sending one out, even if it feels strange at first. There is nothing more chic than being the kind of person who sends a note after someone has served you a nice dinner.

THANKS!

Just a little note to say

Merci Beaucoup!

HOW TO WRITE A LETTER
ABOUT NOTHING AT ALL

Once you have read enough famous letters of roiling passions and poise in the face of modern life's cruelty, you might feel cowed into never writing a letter at all. If you are not scribbling in a violent heat, moaning that your audience is "food and drink to me—the whole bloody machinery," as Henry Miller once wrote Anaïs Nin in history's horniest epistle, why even clutch your pen?

Well, one of the great joys about letters is that they do not have to be about *anything* at all. They don't even have to be good or wise. They just have to keep the volley afloat with their addressee. A correspondence is more dance than posture, so lower your expectations and embrace the great joy of the postbag: the letter about nothing.

To write a letter about nothing, just start. The only way to fail to write a letter about nothing is to not write a letter at all, which is somehow less than nothing. Perhaps start with something you see out your window or a joke you've heard. It might seem like low material, but the poet James Schuyler once wrote to Frank O'Hara, "Why did the nothing keep doing nothing? Because he had nothing to do." If it's good enough for some of the finest wordsmiths of the twentieth century, it's good enough for you.

From there, just let your mind unfold. Use your boredom as an excuse to try something new. Perhaps, the dramas of everyday life have formed a rut in your interests. Maybe there is a word that you've just learned, such as *bathetic* and you want to give it a go. You can think of correspondence as a training arena for new turns of phrase, in which no one is going to say, "That's not actually what that means." It's in a letter, so it's intentional. Maybe they just didn't get it! Maybe you can even get meta and fill your letter with regrets about writing a lengthy note about nothing. This shows your addressee that you care about them enough to respect their time, but also that you want to spend as much of it with them as possible, even if only over the page.

Warning: Letters about nothing have a tendency to turn into ruminations on emptiness, absence, loneliness, or loss. If you find yourself going in this direction, you may want to pull up the yoke. That's dangerously close to a letter about *something* and it may deserve more delicacy than the smattering of assorted jokes, quotes, and linguistic cul-de-sacs suggested above. Then, again, maybe a "bathetic" frame can give you the relief you need to take on the big topics.

SINCERELY CONSIDER . . .

Writing about Your Morning Routine

Yes, we all wake up in the morning (well, if we're lucky). Yes, our daily rituals—the soggy bowls of overnight oats, the hot shower ablutions, the choosing of undergarments—are banal and, for the most part, boring as hell. So, get it out of your system. Write about what you had for breakfast. Is it great content? Not really. But sometimes there might be more lurking at the bottom of the cereal bowl than you were expecting.

On Stamps

At some point, during the height of the early pandemic, I became delirious and stir-crazy enough to believe that perhaps I should get into stamp collecting. I was writing a lot of letters, and I found myself gazing for several minutes at each new stamp on the envelopes I received, marveling at their variety and beauty (reader: I had been inside way too long). I figured that all signs were pointing to me becoming an amateur philatelist, and so I ordered a stamp-collecting kit online from a creaky, lo-fi website that looked like it had not been updated since the nineties. I soon found myself in possession of a giant, puffy plastic three-ring binder that came with several gummy pages made for storing rare stamps, along with a thick guide explaining in extreme detail every aspect of the trade, from how to spot fake three-cent Washingtons from swindlers and how to locate the best first-day covers at a stamp convention, to how to keep your rare Inverted Jenny stamps in pristine mint condition. After flipping through the guide, I felt both impressed with its rigor and also fully convinced that the philatelic life was not for me. The binder ended up languishing on a low shelf, unused and unloved. Of course, I see the basic appeal of collecting stamps. It is a noble and time-honored hobby, dating back to the 1800s, and one that has captured the hearts and minds of millions. Amelia Earhart was a philatelist; so were George Bernard Shaw, Freddie Mercury, John Lennon, and Queen Elizabeth II. There are so many stamps to collect—over 4,000 different varieties issued in the United States alone since 1847—and there are always more appearing all the time. It is a nearly bottomless pursuit, and you could spend a lifetime trying to scoop them all up like lickable Pokémon. But I realized that I am far more interested in using stamps than in preserving them like fossils—and as this is a book about writing and sending letters, it is also, in some way, a book about finding and using stamps.

Stamps are quite incredible, as far as little squares of paper go. They are both legal currency and small works of art, historical objects that also happen to make it possible to put a letter in a mailbox and have it end up on the other side of the country. When I was a child, I was entranced by an old Sesame Street segment called "I Am a Letter" that followed a piece of mail as it made its way through the postal system, particularly the part where the cancellation machine thwacked a postmark over the stamp, signifying that the stamp had fulfilled its purpose. Later, as an adult, I found myself regularly scrolling through the website Mystic Stamps, which sells and catalogs every stamp issued in the United States along with detailed history about the making of the stamp and the artist who designed it, late at night when I could not sleep. What I love about stamps is that they never stop being useful, even as the price of postage rises (an eight-cent stamp still counts for eight cents worth of postage, even if it is fifty years old). This means that the entire back catalog of thousands and thousands of stamps is technically available for you to use on your letters. You can still mail a letter today with a stamp that was issued in 1900, or 1920, or 1970. As long as it has never been mailed before, any old stamp is still perfectly viable (though, unless they are old "forever" stamps, you'll need to carefully calculate how many to use to add up to the current postage rate).

Once you get into the world of vintage stamps, it can be addictive. At one point, I was ordering so many from one seller on eBay that I started to refer to him as my "stamp guy" (shout out to Stuart Katz Stamps & Coins in Hampton, New Hampshire!). I eventually cut back, but I still replenish my stash of vintage stamps once or twice a year, just to have a little something extra to splash onto envelopes.

SO, YOU WANT TO GET INTO VINTAGE STAMPS . . .

1. **START BY SCROLLING**: Sites like Mystic Stamp Company and HipStamp, along with the Smithsonian and the Postal Museum, are terrific resources for looking through the archive and finding stamps that match your moods or interests, or just looking back through history for inspiration. I sometimes like to look through all the stamps from a given year and then pick one or two that I want to add to my rotation. Because there are almost 5,000 stamps to choose from, you will never run out of options. No matter how you are feeling or what you are into, there is a stamp for that. There are stamps featuring, but certainly not limited to: classic movie stars, jazz musicians, rescue dogs, antique dolls, muscle cars, vaudeville comedians, mariachi singers, skyscrapers, cloud formations, famous novelists, civil rights leaders, nocturnal mammals, ice cream, movie posters of Black cinema classics, scientists, choreographers, sneakers, coffee drinks, children's cartoons, blown glass, opera divas, and tennis balls. You must become a cartographer of your whims! Let yourself seek out the obscure old stamp that speaks to you.

2. **FIND A RESELLER**: You can find many places to buy old stamps online, and prices vary wildly. There are major dealers that are reliable and vetted for collectors, but I find the costs to be higher than those on eBay or Etsy (if you are looking to use your stamps and not preserve them, then you can afford to gamble a bit). The cost of vintage stamps is constantly fluctuating based on demand. You can often find a sheet of stamps for half the price just by scrolling around between various sites and comparison shopping. Think of it as a scavenger hunt.

3. **BUY THE CHEAPEST STAMPS IN BUNDLES**: You can regularly find sellers offering mixed bundles of three, four, or five cent stamps by the hundreds. Good to buy once so that you always have a wacky stamp at the ready to add on as a flourish.

4. **STORE YOUR LOOSE STAMPS IN A TACKLE BOX.** That's it, that's the entire tip. A basic fly-fishing tackle box has perfect-sized compartments in which to store stacks of stamps.

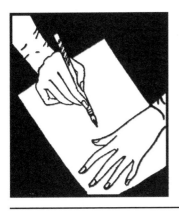

Writing Prompts

WRITE A DETAILED ACCOUNT of the last time you got food poisoning. Do you know what the culprit was? Did you have a sinking feeling that eating three-day-old shrimp was a terrible idea? Go into the gory timeline. Spare no detail or humiliation. Channel an old *Seventeen* magazine "Traumarama" column.

MOST PUBLISHED ESSAYS should really just be letters between friends who can poke at each other's embryonic ideas in the safety of their rapport. Choose an issue that you're trying to figure out and attempt to compose your thoughts. The long feedback time really gives you a chance to sit with your opinions as well as your friend's reactions to them. This short-circuits a lot of our rhetorical defenses and forces us to actually consider an idea as someone else might.

THAT OLD-SAW QUESTION about three dead people you would invite to a dinner party is tired . . . but you can revive it in your letters. Nobody cares if it has all been done before! So . . . who are you inviting over for negronis and a summer salad in your fantasies? What would they talk about? Who will you seat at the head of the table?

SPRITZ SOME PERFUME on the page and then spend a few paragraphs describing the scent—your very own DIY scratch-n-sniff adventure.

A CLASSIC GENRE OF LOVE LETTER is "If you were here, I would do this to you." Though this form has been eagerly adapted and abridged by contemporary sexters, consider a more quotidian counterfactual. Send a cross-continental friend a fantasy of a perfect shared afternoon. Detail the beats of a road trip that you are manifesting.

WHAT IS A SECRET SKILL you possess that you rarely get to flex? Flex it all the way in your next letter. Don't hold back. Explain why you just might be the best floral arranger or furniture assembler or amateur origami artist that no one has ever heard of. Pretend that you are your own publicist.

MAKE YOUR OWN MAD LIB. Everyone loves a Mad Lib. It may seem hokey at first, but once you get the hang of it, it's a barrel of _____.
                   (animal, plural)

WHAT DO YOU COLLECT? How did you begin your collection? Is it something you're open about or is it a secret you can only share in the context of a letter (perhaps the world isn't ready to understand your antique teaspoon collection, but, one day, they will).

WHAT IS THE TELEVISION SHOW you watch the most when you have the flu/a dissociative afternoon/the need to turn your brain off? Can you quote it from memory?

WATCH A MOVIE and write down all the things you'd whisper to your friend in the theater as they occur to you. Then, have your pen pal read the letter while they are watching the same movie and repeat the exercise. By the time this film makes its round trip, it will have acquired mythic significance in your friendship, no matter how good or bad it actually is.

WHAT WAS YOUR MOST EXTRAVAGANT impulse purchase and just how much credit card debt did you go into as a result?

COME UP WITH A NICKNAME for your correspondent and address every letter to them using it from now on, without commenting on the fact that you are doing it. Just start addressing your letters "Dear Marshmallow" or "Dear Miss Monday" or "Dear Turtle" or "Dear Sparkles" or whatever feels right. Conversely, come up with a unique sign-off and stick to it. The writer Lucia Berlin signed her letters "Loosha" to playfully refer to the phonetic pronunciation of her first name. What will be your Loosha?

WRITE A LETTER out of breath. Go for a run or do some yoga or heavy lifting and then scribble a card to a confidante. There's a certain slow, thoughtful letter-writing posture we often assume when "sitting down to write." What happens to your letters when your heart's racing and you're dripping sweat on the stamp?

THROW A DINNER PARTY and write to a friend who cannot attend about how ludicrous your social circle is. Half of the Austenian letter catalog are meditations on the asinine conversations that the author took part in. Why should our regency betters get to have all the fun? Worried that your gently mocked compatriots will discover your letters? Even better. Now you have the basis for a plot!

TAKE POLAROIDS of your life for an entire week. Send them in an envelope with messages on the back of each one on a Post-it note (number the photos for proper sequencing).

WRITE A SERIES OF LETTERS while sitting on public benches: At the park, describe the people who walk past. Inside a museum, describe the art you see while sitting down. Outside a coffee shop, describe the dogs that trot by.

WHAT'S YOUR NUMBER-ONE LIFE HACK, the one you share with everyone you know? Where were you when you discovered that the little arrow symbol next to the symbol of a gas tank on a car's dashboard tells you which side to pump gas on? When did you learn about changing your Gmail settings so that you have a full minute to un-send that 2 a.m. email to your ex? Pass along some everyday wisdom.

WHAT'S ONE THING you do that costs less than $50 and makes your life feel more glamorous? Make yourself a persnickety little tea service in the afternoon? Put twinkle lights up in your windows? Make your own salt scrubs? Give the gift of spilling your best madcap-on-a-budget tips.

WRITE A LETTER that is just your favorite sentences from the last five books you read.

YEARNING FOR LOVE is well-covered territory. Write a letter about yearning for something that is completely trivial, but totally desired. Spin yourself into a frenzy thinking about gelato. Pour yourself into the mouth of a sample sale. We deceive ourselves into thinking that we are our grandest ambitions, but more often than not we are our tiniest fetishes.

IMAGINE THAT, years after your death, some cineaste makes a documentary about your time on earth and they need a letter representative of contemporary attitudes to voice over in a friendly, colloquial cant. Write the letter that you'd be most tickled to hear booming out of a pan-and-zoom montage.

DRAW A MAP of a well-trod stroll you often take through your city. Label the best place to get croissants and the place where you do laundry hungover or get your shoes cobbled. Bonus points if you create coordinates and then write an entire letter about places where the axes intersect . . . "At E6 is the coffee shop where an ex broke up with me because I was 'too good at karaoke,' while at B3 you'll find the corner where I once sat on the curb and ate nearly an entire pizza while crying with a friend on speakerphone." Be the deranged tour guide of your own urban history.

FOR THE MOST PART, music is meant to be shared, but the convenience of an iPhone with every second of recorded history often makes our daily streaming a lonely affair. Write a letter that's a listening session with a friend. Dig into how each song makes you feel. Mercilessly skip an overlong interlude. Let your friend experience an album through you.

WAIT UNTIL YOU HIT A PEAK of boredom. (As a sidenote, if you find that you never get bored, try removing all the chattering little devices from your life until the tedium hits.) Now, write a letter in this state of dull detachment. At first, you'll fear that you have nothing to say, but soon enough you will do anything to amuse yourself and, often, this will amuse your recipient as well.

IF YOU'VE EVER SPENT TIME on a country porch or in a rural social enclosure of any type, you know how much old-timers love to complain about bodily aches and pains. Go long on how your fragile body is failing you. The archives are full of masters of letters bitching about a bad back. Join the proud and slumped tradition.

TURN OUT ALL THE LIGHTS and burn a candle. Practice letter-writing as meditation. Try to translate your calm into your lines. It might feel like a silly séance, but for how much of recorded history was this the normal way to do your correspondence? Does a dimming light and a rhythmic flicker attune you any differently to your task?

ORDER A FRENCH 75 (or a lemonade) and park yourself at an outdoor table in the middle of a busy sidewalk. List all of the things you witness and attach your wry social commentary. People-watching is among the great shared pastimes, but it can be just as enjoyable as an asynchronous pursuit. You have more time to fashion devastating critiques of ill-fitting blazers and questionable dog parenting.

WRITE A LETTER about your worst boss. Your worst job. Your worst fashion mistake. Your worst haircut. Your worst public speaking disaster. Your worst kiss. Your worst cooking experiment. Your worst attempt at flirting. Your worst party foul. Relive all of the lowlights; really revel in them. Misery loves epistolary company.

WRITE A LETTER in the second person. This is an interesting technique in fiction, but even more arresting when the "you" is a specific "you." There's a formal intimacy there that could really unlock something with a game interlocutor.

WRITE A LETTER and then cut it up into jigsaw puzzle pieces. It's obnoxious, sure, but it will make your recipient feel like they have just received a ransom note in a Liam Neeson movie. An experience everyone should have at least once.

GET DRESSED UP to write a letter. The letter doesn't have to be about how you feel in your clothing, how the right dress transforms your perception of the world, but that can be a great place to start. Our friends so often get notes born of sweatpants and pajamas. What kind of letter comes out of silk? What is the correspondence of lace?

DRAW A TAROT CARD in the morning. Write a letter about what you think it all means. Read *a lot* into it. Burn some incense while you're writing. Wear whatever outfit you have (preferably velvet) that makes you feel the most like you can predict the future.

EMBRACE THE LETTER as a form of poetry. This is not to say that you should include actual poems in your letters, but consider the letter as a piece of poetry. The New York School was constantly writing and publishing letters between themselves that blurred the line between simple epistles and postmarked free verse. How would one of your letters change if you thought of it as a literary work?

BUY THE UGLIEST-COLORED INK you can find. I'm talking shimmering garbage, dichromatic puce and olive, neon Velveeta orange. You should feel calligraphic dysmorphia as you are writing. Go against all of your aesthetic impulses when crafting the envelope. Ask yourself, "Can arranging stamps be an act of malice?" You might surprise yourself with the letter that comes out. Sometimes all we need to push ourselves into new territories is a home that does not feel like home.

WRITE A LETTER that is just five copied sentences from the best books you read last year. Cite your sources, maybe explain why the passages resonated with you. Or not! Let the authors do the talking.

START A VERY SLOW DIALOGUE. Send your friend several pages, with only a paragraph. Encourage them to add on and send it back. This is something between an exquisite corpse and a chat room over the laggiest Internet. Over time your letter will take on wear and weight. It will become a seasoned artifact, patina-ed in the post. Eventually, someone will have to choose to keep it or it might get lost. *C'est la vie.*

WRITE A LETTER that's one long, single sentence. Do not explain yourself. You don't need to make excuses for your stylistic choices. The right recipient will understand its intent.

How to Write a Letter about Nothing at All

HOW TO READ
A LETTER

Sending a letter is a generous act; reading a letter should be no less so. The best way to read a letter is the way you hope your letters will be read—without distractions, with an open mind, maybe in a bubble bath. I like to schedule a few times a week to really dig into the letters I have received (this is partially due to volume—as a result of my pen pal project and other correspondences I have fostered over the years, I get somewhere between ten and twenty letters a week). I always set aside separate times for reading letters and responding to them—I find that if you read a letter and write back immediately, you often find yourself responding, bullet-point style, to everything the person said without offering much creativity of your own. I believe in allowing for a few days of breathing room in between getting a letter and responding to it, just to let the note rattle around. Sometimes I'll carry a letter with me as I move around the city, reading bits of it on the subway or a park bench or while I'm waiting for a friend. The key is to make a ritual out of it!

Here are a few quick suggestions for letter-reading rituals you might want to try:

Read all of your letters in the bath, like Seymour Glass in Salinger's Franny and Zooey. *Yes, your letters WILL get waterlogged. Yes, you will drop one by accident and ruin it at some point. Doesn't matter. You're an original.*

Read your letters while eating alone at a bar. Order one glass of wine or good sparkling water, the pasta dish that speaks to you, and read by the light of that one sad votive candle they put out for you.

Select a big chair in your apartment. The BEST chair. Always read letters there while listening to opera arias. Or Spanish guitar. Or a film score. Or bouncy jazz. Something that makes the whole experience feel cinematic and urbane, like a stylish director might be secretly filming it from behind a plant.

𝕷𝖎𝖌𝖍𝖙 𝖎𝖓𝖈𝖊𝖓𝖘𝖊 or a too-expensive candle and read your letters while sitting on a floor pillow or draped across a chaise like a depressive beauty from a pre-Raphaelite painting.

Recite your letters out loud, pacing around the room. Read them to your dog or cat. They won't judge.

Letters make great plane and train reading. Take them with you on a long journey (I've been known to bring letters on vacation).

Pick an hour and a beverage—first thing in the morning, with coffee, or in the afternoon with Earl Grey, or very late, with a nightcap or a cocoa—and always pair the two when you read your correspondence. Be consistent and persnickety about it. Call it your "reading period." Hold it sacrosanct.

PARIS-LYON

4 H.50

AUTOMOTRICE RAPIDE BUGATTI
1re & 2me CLASSES

PARIS	8h	LYON	18h50
LAROCHE	9h31	DIJON	20h39
DIJON	10h56	LAROCHE	22h04
LYON	12h49	PARIS	23h40

SAUF DIMANCHES & FÊTES

Letter Collections for Your Bookshelf

Letters are, for the most part, intended to be private affairs. This is what makes them perpetually alluring as a form of communication, when so much of our lives are public—they are analog arenas in which to work out your thoughts without the fear that your words might be shared or intercepted (unless you are somehow living out a Shakespeare tragedy or a Vaudevillian farce, in which case you have every right to fear that your letters might fall into the wrong hands). There is a sacred, unspoken aura around a letter; it is for one person to read and tuck away, keeping your words and petty gripes in the mutual emotional vault. That is, of course, unless you happen to be a person of some notoriety, or if you are no longer alive—and if you're both famous and dead, then the chances are very good that your very private letters have made their way into the pages of an anthology. But . . . you're likely past caring at that point.

For the rest of us, letter collections, while existing in the ethical gray area where privacy and publishing commingle, are undeniably delightful to read. Letters, when they were the hottest communication method going, just used to be better. That's the simple truth. Not only were they written with candor and passion and raw feeling and righteous fury, but they were written with style. It was in letters that people could be their truest selves; where writers were at their funniest, their cruelest, their most flirtatious, their most beautifully confused and searching.

I have been gathering letter collections for years

not only because they remind me how to read (if you are ever in a book rut, grab a book of letters from the shelf—you can read each one like a little snack and it will reengage your reading appetite), but because they teach me how to write, particularly when my tank feels completely empty. When you see how eloquent, silly, and complicated people could be in their writing for just one other person, it pushes you to strengthen your own compositional muscle. Perhaps the general quality of letters flung into the world has diminished now that they are an anachronism, but that doesn't mean your letters have to be any less worthy of posthumous publication than those of the greats. Reading great letters makes you want to write great letters. At the very least, they tend to be full of messy entanglements and human failings. It is a way to see the unpolished and unfettered thoughts of your favorite writers; it is getting to listen in while they talk to their friends.

I cannot recommend enough building up a library of letter (and, sometimes, email) collections. I encourage you to seek out strange and unexpected titles for yourself. There are hundreds to find, many of which are out of print and waiting for you in a dollar bin. Most used bookstores have a dusty letter collection somewhere in the back, and I find they tend to be overflowing with treasures. Go hunting!

HOW TO MAKE FRIENDS AND CORRESPOND WITH PEOPLE

I live in the real world; I know it is not 1895 and you are not stuck at your desk every night, tending to your correspondence under the glow of a spermaceti oil lamp, scribbling away with a heavy dip pen and a well of slippery India ink. I mean, you might very well be that person, but you and I both know that writing and mailing physical letters in the twenty-first century is more or less a form of vintage cosplay. We have email. We have smartphones. We have DMs. We can 3D-print entire cars. People used to send letters abroad to announce many months in advance that they would be making a journey; now, you can text someone when you land in a new country and have dinner plans sorted before you go through customs. There is something fantastically inefficient about sending a letter, and certainly a bit absurd. A letter currently serves no function as a way to transmit important information or even to keep in touch with people; if you are really close with someone, you huddle via group text or over coffee, not through the postal service. And yet, there is something both freeing and a little bit dangerous about engaging with a dead form of communication. It feels both crucial and cringe; like an urgent and daffy performance in order to keep the medium alive. Letter-writing is nearly extinct, and keeping it going requires purpose and passion and, sure, a bit of delusion. And it requires you to have someone to write to.

Finding other people who want to write letters back and forth in this mostly letter-less world can be a challenge. You are essen-

tially asking someone to engage with you in a long game of make-believe that might end up being very meaningful. This is why I always tell people that you cannot be shy about your intentions when it comes to starting up a correspondence. It's an essentially humbling ask, but once you put yourself out there, you will find there are others who will take up the call. If you have social media, start there. It saves you the acute stress of asking a specific friend if they want to start corresponding the archaic way. They might take you up on it, but then again, they might not, and now the whistling, empty canyon of a rejected pen pal–ship will haunt you.

Before I started my pandemic letter-writing experiment, I would often go on Twitter and simply ask people to DM me if they wanted to start writing letters. Many of the people who responded were total strangers, which I found to be a relief; there's no lower-pressure activity than sending off random thoughts to someone across the country you will absolutely never run into in real life. Use Instagram, Twitter, Facebook, bat signal, whatever you prefer. Simply say: I just got my hands on some great stationery/postcards/a new pen and I really want to send some snail mail. Let me know if you have an empty mailbox! (Truly, you can use this exact script, I gift it to you.) After you've canvassed your followers for takers, then you can start going through your rolodex. I like to start with old friends or colleagues or mentors who live far away and maybe you haven't spoken to in a few years, though they were once dear to you; the kind of friends you would send a holiday card or a birth announcement to—let them know that you are writing them a letter to catch up, and then really do it. They might not volley back, but often these blast-from-the-past letters are the most appreciated (this is how I began one of my favorite correspondences with an old teacher of mine). Next, try family. Funky aunts and distant cousins. The goal is to just *start*, with one or two people, and you will quickly find that correspondences start falling into your life. Once you are the kind of person who writes letters, suddenly you find a lot more people who want to receive a letter from you.

How to End a Correspondence

Sometimes a letter exchange just . . . isn't working. Perhaps the letters have gotten stale and routine, the two of you just tossing back and forth the same blah sentences full of superficial information over and over. Perhaps the rhythm is just off (either you or the other person wants to write more often or cannot keep up with the pace). Perhaps you're just not feeling it! It's one thing to have a fiery and contentious, even barbed, exchange with a mind you respect (see the collected letters of pretty much any author); it's another to have uninspiring and lackluster correspondence chemistry. Letters are an alchemical thing. You know when it isn't right.

The easiest way to end a correspondence, and the way most people choose to do it, is simply by not writing back. We live in a fast-paced time, and it is easy to lose track of slow forms of communication. You can easily ditch someone when your only contact is through the USPS. I am not against this method if your correspondence is truly at a standstill—if you both have lost the spark, there's a high likelihood that both parties will feel some relief with a no-nonsense ghosting. This method is also the one to use if someone's letters have started to feel a bit uncomfortable or invasive (no need to ever engage in a correspondence that makes you feel unsafe or unhappy; this is an elective hobby, after all). But the Houdini method is quite gauche to use if (1) you know the person well outside of a letter-writing context (AKA a family member, someone who started as your real-life friend first, or a pen pal you've since met and befriended) or (2) if the person is still writing you lively and engaged updates and has really done nothing wrong, other than keeping the letters coming when you no longer feel in sync.

My first recommendation for tapering off an otherwise benevolent correspondence is to suggest a lower-commitment postcard exchange instead (you can even do this via postcard, to get it going). I did this nearly ten years back with a friend during a time when I was not feeling up to writing a lot, and we still send each other postcards from our travels. If you really just want to end the correspondence outright, you can always send a kind letter explaining that you just don't feel you have the time to be a great pen pal at the moment (the classic "It's not you, it's me" tactic). This said, you can always offer to write again when you feel up to it in the future. Letters are supposed to be fun! Nobody is demanding that you mail them things! Take six months off if you need to! Take a year! Perhaps you'll return to your correspondence with fresh energy. And if your postal breakup really does stick . . . it was for the best. Sometimes, you have to lick a lot of envelopes to find your letter-writing soul mate.

HOW TO STORE YOUR LETTERS AND REVISIT THEM

When I started writing letters, coming up with a "correspondence storage system" wasn't really at the forefront of my mind. I am not a naturally organized person to begin with, and I figured that I would place any letters I needed to respond to in a nubby little stack on my desk. As I began writing more, however, and the influx increased—at the height of the PenPalooza project, I got between ten and fifteen letters a day; I still get around two or three every day now—I realized that I needed a way to manage the flow.

If you have several correspondents, I suggest buying one of those old-school office trays that divides ingoing and outgoing memos and use it to organize the letters you need to respond to (if you are better at executive functioning than I am, you might even do so chronologically, in the order in which you need to respond). I have a small notebook on my desk in which I note down the day I receive a letter—I then cross off the letter when I respond to it and add the reply date.

Regardless of your letter-writing cadence and the way you choose to manage your outgoing mail, you should be storing the letters you receive for posterity. Handwritten letters are archival materials that we are creating in real time, and you should treat

them that way. I recommend buying a set of pretty boxes that you are excited to use (you can find stacking boxes online, printed with flowers or abstract designs; I also like vintage hatboxes or leftover shoeboxes that you can cover with nice wrapping paper) and lining them with acid-free tissue paper, which will help preserve your letters and keep them from yellowing or drying out over the years. Keep them on a high shelf in a cool, dry place, away from pets or pests. Do not bind your letters together with rubber bands or twine—as romantic as it is to think of your grandchildren finding a cache of your old love letters tied up in a neat little bundle, the pressure will weaken the paper over time.

But, and this is my best tip: Don't just leave them sitting there, untouched, for years and years. Letters are living history, emphasis on the *living*. Pull the boxes down from time to time and rifle through them. Pick out an old letter and reread it. Shuffle through the letters and see if there is someone you have lost touch with. Consider replying three years late to a letter whose breadcrumb trail has gone cold. It's silly and awkward and marvelous to read your old letters.

Lastly, if you really want to create an archive that future generations can enjoy and get to know you through, even if you have been gone for centuries (note my cautious optimism that humanity will still be around for hundreds of years . . .) it cannot just be one-sided. I would tell you to Xerox your outgoing mail and file it away, but nobody has a Xerox machine at home these days—instead, take a picture of what you write on your phone and save it to a private folder on your computer.

Someday, someone might want to read the letters you wrote without having to track down all of your correspondents for the evidence. It may seem cumbersome and counterintuitive now, but one day, you (or your great-great-great niece) might be grateful for it. And, as a bonus, if your letter does get lost on its way to its destination, you have a backup copy you can print out or send along.

CONCLUSION

※

WHY WE WRITE
LETTERS AND MUST
KEEP DOING IT!

DEAR READER,

I have something to confess to you (because what are letters for, if not confessions?). So, lean closer: Many times when I was working on this book, I fell into what I have taken to calling the Chasm of Doubt. I had late nights where I wondered if the subject of letter-writing was frivolous, or aggressively antiquated, or at the very least out of step from an increasingly complex and confusing world where very little can be solved by putting a wax seal on an envelope. As a journalist, I try to focus on what is happening right now and attempt to make some sense of it—and yet here I was, staying up until 2 a.m. to research the history of onion skin paper and pore over rare stamps. Not exactly hard-hitting news. And yet, every time I went into a spiral or even thought about abandoning this project, what brought me right back to it was the act of sitting down at my desk and writing a letter to someone.

Very little has made me feel more connected to people—and to the world we live in—than carrying on years-long correspondences with dozens of total strangers who I might otherwise have never known, who have allowed me into their mailboxes and into their lives, who have shared with me their secrets and in turn have held mine, and who have been honest and bold on the page.

It is always funny to me that this book project has its roots in social media, because in so many ways, writing letters over the last few years has been my pathway out of the vice grip of the endless scroll. Correspondence is slow by nature, but that does not mean it cannot keep up with the times—if anything, I've found that gobbling down Internet memes for hours on end makes me feel dead inside; it is when I pull out a pen and start to answer a letter that I feel myself snapping back into the present moment (and not for nothing, but handwritten letters are going to be one of the very last things that our AI overlords can take from us).

So yes, maintaining a correspondence may seem outmoded. Writing in longhand might feel bizarre and it might give you an unsightly finger callus. You may not know what to say, or how to say it, and you might feel like you're pretending to be the kind of person who writes letters rather than fully embodying the role. But for all of its ties to an obsolete past, letter writing has been my conduit for envisioning a more intimate, more empathetic, and more authentically connected future.

I think of the words of the late Argentinian writer Ricardo Piglia, who in his 1980 novella *Respiración Artificial*, wrote that "correspondence is the utopian form of conversation because it annihilates the present and turns the future into the only possible place for dialogue." I think he was trying to say that writing a letter is an inherently hopeful act: You hope that it will arrive, you hope that it will be read, you hope that you will receive a reply. Of course, all along this chain of hoping, any number of factors— a rainstorm that smudges an address, an envelope that falls between the cracks of a postal sorter, a sticky-fingered neighbor who swipes your mail—can thwart your plans, but such is life. We keep going anyway. All you have is right now, this paper, this desk, and this letter you have to write.

I'm not by any means suggesting that dropping a letter into the mail will change the world, but I do believe that it might change you—and it will certainly change your relationship to people, and to time. Letters require you to wait. They require you to live with uncertainty and impatience. Epistolary relationships require a lot of patience and flexibility. But also—and most important— writing letters is a good time. It is a chance to be creative and weird, to learn how to emboss paper or use a fountain pen, to go hunting for strange old postcards and flat ephemera, to do your very best to elicit surprise and wonder in the receiver. It's something you do for yourself and for someone else at the same time, and on either side the goal is connection and delight.

So. Go write a letter. It need not be intricate or long, or even more than a few lines. If you don't have someone to write to, start asking around. Ask friends, ask family, ask acquaintances. Join a pen pal exchange. Start a pen pal exchange. Write to your mother, or to your sibling, or to your oldest friend. Once you start making it known that you want to write letters, you might be surprised at who emerges to answer the call. Write your letters promiscuously. Some correspondences will fizzle and fade, others will bloom over time; some will click right away, and some will never feel quite right. Keep going. "A letter always arrives at its destination." Enjoy yourself, write with abandon, play around with the medium, make it your own. I can guarantee that you will arrive somewhere new.

XOX,

Rachel Syme

NOTES

INTRODUCTION: A LETTER FROM RACHEL

1   **"FORGET THE PAST":** F. Scott Fitzgerald to Zelda Fitzgerald, 1934, in *Dear Scott, Dearest Zelda: The Love Letters of F. Scott and Zelda Fitzgerald*, eds. Jackson R. Breyer and Cathy W. Barks (London: Bloomsbury, 2002). Ebook.

1   **WHILE IN SPAIN:** Diana Vreeland papers, Manuscripts, Archives, and Rare Books Division, the New York Public Library.

DEAR READER

10   **FROST'S ORIGINAL LETTER-WRITER:** S. Annie Frost, *Frost's Original Letter-Writer* (New York: Dick & Fitzgerald, 1897).

10   **"COLD WATER REFRESHES":** S. Annie Frost, *Frost's Laws and by-Laws of American Society* (New York: Dick & Fitzgerald, 1896), 158.

11   **"ANSWERING AN ADVERTISEMENT FOR A CHAMBERMAID":** S. Annie Frost, *Frost's Original Letter-Writer* (New York: Dick & Fitzgerald, 1897), 5.

11   **"QUOTATIONS SHOULD BE USED":** Frost, *Original Letter-Writer*, 26.

11   **"NEVER WRITE IN PENCIL":** Frost, *Original Letter-Writer*, 32.

11   **"STINGY LITTLE PET":** Frost, *Original Letter-Writer*, 127.

HOW TO BE A PEN PAL

20   **"EXCLUSIVE CLUB STARTED IN THE LATE 1920S":** Joan Reardon, ed., *As Always, Julia: The Letters of Julia Child and Avis DeVoto* (New York: Harper Collins, 2011). Ebook.

20   **"I HOPE YOU WON'T MIND HEARING"** and all other excerpts from the letters of Avis de Voto: Papers of Avis De Voto collection, call number A-167, Schlesinger Library, Radcliffe Institute, Harvard University. Permissions courtesy Mark De Voto.

20   **"THIS AFTERNOON WE START FOR THE WILD WEST":** Willa Cather, "#0041: Willa Cather to George Seibel and Helen Hiller Seibel, August 9, [1897]," *The Complete Letters of Willa Cather*, ed. Willa Cather Archive team. The Willa Cather Archive, 2018. Accessed June 7, 2024.

21   **JULIA CHILD WAS A LATE BLOOMER:** Bob Spitz, *Dearie: The Remarkable Life of Julia Child* (New York: Vintage, 2003).

HOW TO WRITE YOUR VERY FIRST LETTER

23   **"LETTERS ARE ABOVE ALL USEFUL":** Elizabeth Hardwick, *The Collected Essays of Elizabeth Hardwick* (New York: NYRB Classics, 2017). Ebook.

HOW TO WRITE A FAN LETTER

25   **GEORGE CLOONEY APPARENTLY WRITES LETTERS EVERY DAY:** Jordan Hoffman, "George Clooney, Man of Letters," *Vanity Fair*, December 19, 2020, https://www.vanityfair.com/hollywood/2020/12/george-clooney-man-of-letters.

25   **PRINCE WROTE LETTERS TO JONI MITCHELL:** Tim Coffman, "Why Joni Mitchell's Office Intercepted Letters from Prince," *Far Out Magazine*, May 27, 2023, https://faroutmagazine.co.uk/joni-mitchell-office-intercepted-letters-from-prince/.

25   **IN THE 1960S, NINA SIMONE:** "Nina Simone Writes an Admiring Letter to Langston Hughes." *Open Culture*, August 24, 2020, https://www.openculture.com/2020/08/nina-simone-writes-an-admiring-letter-to-langston-hughes.html.

27   **"THE THRILL WAS IN MY WRITING":** Rachel Bedard, "The Case for Writing Fan Mail," *The New York Times*, August 16, 2022.

27   **"HI COMING LATER HEAT THE SOUP":** Tove Jansson, *The Woman Who Borrowed Memories: Selected Stories* (New York: NYRB Classics, 2014). Ebook.

HOW TO WRITE ABOUT THE WEATHER

30   **"I HAVE A WEEK'S VACATION":** Willa Cather, "#0103: Willa Cather to Viola Roseboro', February 19, [1905]" in *The Complete Letters of Willa Cather*, ed. Willa Cather Archive team. The Willa Cather Archive, 2018. Accessed June 7, 2024.

31   **"FOR NO PARTICULAR REASON"** and **"WE ARE HAVING A GLORIOUS SUMMER":** Bessie Head, in *Everyday Matters: Selected Letters of Dora Taylor, Bessie Head & Lilian Ngoyi*, ed. Margaret J. Daymond (South Africa: Jacana, 2015). Reproduced with permission of Johnson & Alcock Ltd., London, on behalf of the Estate of Bessie Head. Copyright © Bessie Head.

32   **"PRESENTLY WE SHALL WALK"** Reproduced with permission of Curtis Brown Group Ltd., London on behalf of the Beneficiaries of the Estate of Vita Sackville-West. Copyright © Vita Sackville-West.

TO EVERY LETTER, THERE IS A SEASON

34   **"SUMMER BILLOWS," "VAPOROUS HEAT," "THREATENED TO HATCH":** Zelda Fitzgerald to F. Scott Fitzgerald, in *Dear Scott, Dearest Zelda: The Love Letters of F. Scott and Zelda Fitzgerald*, eds., Jackson R. Breyer and Cathy W. Barks (London: Bloomsbury, 2002). Ebook.

HOW TO MAIL A RECIPE

41   **"THERE IS SOMETHING TRIUMPHANT":** Laurie Colwin, *Home Cooking: A Writer in the Kitchen* (New York: Vintage, reprinted in 2010). Ebook.

HOW TO WRITE A LETTER LIKE A POET

44   **"MOST OF THEM HAVE BROWN HEADS":** Elizabeth Bishop to Marianne Moore, 1937, in *One Art: Letters* (New York: Farrar Straus and Giroux, 2015), 53.

44   **"HER FEATHERS ARE GRIMY":** Leslie Marmon Silko to James Wright, in *The Delicacy and Strength of Lace: Letters Between Leslie Marmon Silko and James Wright*, ed. Anne Wright (Minneapolis: Graywolf Press, 2009), 37.

44   **IN SYLVIA PLATH'S CASE:** Sylvia Plath, *Letters Home: Correspondence 1950-1963*, ed. Aurelia Schober Plath (New York: Harper Perennial, 1992).

45   **"DEARLY TILLIE":** Anne Sexton to Tillie Olsen, 1965, in *Anne Sexton: A Self Portrait in Letters*, ed. Linda Gray Sexton and Lois Ames (New York: Ecco, 2004). Reprinted by permission of SLL/Sterling Lord Literistic, Inc. Copyright by Linda Gray Sexton, Literary Executor for Anne Sexton.

HOW TO PRESS A FLOWER

52   **IN JAPAN, THE PRACTICE OF OSHIBANA:** Shannon Carr, "Flower Pressing," *Fort Bend Museum*, April 29, 2020, https://www.fortbendmuseum.org/blog/flower-pressing.

52   **FLORIOGRAPHY:** Emma Flint, "The Secret Victorian Language That's Back in Fashion," *BBC*, October, 13, 2022, https://www.bbc.com/culture/article/20221012-the-flowers-that-send-a-hidden-message.

52   **KATE GREENAWAY'S 1884 BESTSELLER:** Kate Greenaway, *Language of Flowers* (Warwickshire, UK: Pook Press, 2013).

53   **LACIE RZ PORTA:** Framed Florals, Brooklyn, NY, https://framedflorals.com/.

TO PERFUME OR NOT PERFUME?

62 **IN AN ISSUE OF** *Good Housekeeping*: Anna Sawyer, "The Etiquette of Correspondence," *Good Housekeeping*, March 16, 1889.

HOW TO WRITE A LETTER ABOUT YOUR DREAMS

66 **"DO YOU FEEL IT IS VERY KIND"** Iris Murdoch to Steeple Aston, 1963, in *Living on Paper: Letters from Iris Murdoch, 1934–1995*, eds. Avril Horner and Anne Rowe (Princeton, NJ: Princeton University Press, 2018), 243. Reproduced with permission of Curtis Brown Group Ltd., London on behalf of the Beneficiaries of The Estate of Iris Murdoch. Copyright © Iris Murdoch.

67 **"YOUR CHARMING BEAVER":** Simone de Beauvoir, *Letters to Sartre*, ed. Quentin Hoare (New York: Arcade, 2012).

SINCERELY CONSIDER . . . *GRIFFIN AND SABINE*

70 **NICK BANTOCK'S NOVEL:** Nick Bantock, *Griffin and Sabine, 25th Anniversary Limited Edition: An Extraordinary Correspondence* (San Francisco: Chronicle, 2016).

CREATING A LETTER-WRITING RITUAL

72 **JOHANNES VERMEER'S** *A Lady Writing*: Johannes Vermeer, *A Lady Writing*, 1665, National Gallery of Art, https://www.nga.gov/collection/art-object-page.46437.html.

72 **KAIGETSUDŌ DOSHIN:** Kaigetsudō Doshin, *Courtesan Writing a Letter*, ca. 1715, Metropolitan Museum of Art, https://www.metmuseum.org/art/collection/search/53444.

72 **ALBERT EDELFELT'S** *Lady Writing a Letter*: Albert Edelfelt, *Lady Writing a Letter*, 1887, Swedish Museum of Art and Design, https://collection.nationalmuseum.se:443/eMP/eMuseumPlus?service=ExternalInterface&module=collection&objectId=19713&viewType=detailView.

73 **GABRIEL METSU'S** *Man Writing a Letter*: Gabriel Metsu, *Man Writing a Letter*, 1664–1666, National Gallery of Ireland, http://onlinecollection.nationalgallery.ie/objects/8708/man-writing-a-letter?ctx=2c71d0d9-cc95-4563-baee-ee6472cd44c2&idx=1.

HOW TO WRITE A LETTER FROM ABROAD

79 **"A BOX OF SALTED WAFERS":** M. F. K. Fisher to Eleanor Friede, 1959, in *M. F. K. Fisher: A Life in Letters*, eds. Marsha Moran, Patrick Moran, and Norah K. Barr (Berkeley, CA: Counterpoint Press, 1997), 166.

79 **"THEY ARE CELEBRATING":** Elizabeth Bishop to Marianne Moore, 1942, in *One Art: Letters* (New York: Farrar Straus and Giroux, 2015). Ebook.

SINCERELY CONSIDER . . . POSTCROSSING

81 **A STUDENT THERE NAMED PAULO MAGALHÃES:** "About Postcrossing," *Postcrossing*, accessed Jun 9, 2024, https://www.postcrossing.com/about/history.

ON AIRMAIL

82 **IN 2007, THE UNITED STATES POSTAL SERVICE:** Kim Bhasin and Dina Spector, "11 Services That the US Post Office Has Already Eliminated," *Business Insider*, August 1, 2012, https://www.businessinsider.com/11-services-that-the-us-post-office-has-already-eliminated-2012-8.

82 **1911, PILOT EARLE OVINGTON:** "Ovington's Bleriot IX and Pequet's Sommer-style Airplanes," *Smithsonian National Postal Museum*, accessed January 9, 2024, https://postalmuseum.si.edu/exhibition/fad-to-fundamental-airmail-in-america-historic-airplanes-the-early-airplanes/ovingtons.

83 **AMELIA EARHART NEVER TECHNICALLY WORKED:** "Amelia Earhart," *Smithsonian National Postal Museum*, accessed January 9, 2024, https://postalmuseum.si.edu/exhibition/fad-to-fundamental-airmail-in-america-airmail-pilot-stories-mail-by-female.

83 **RUTH LAW AND KATHERINE STINSON:** "Pioneering Female Aviators," *The Henry Ford Museum*, accessed June 9, 2024, https://www.thehenryford.org/collections-and-research/digital-collections/expert-sets/101266/.

83 **LAW WAS FORCED INTO EARLY RETIREMENT:** Dorothy Cochrane and P. Ramirez, "Ruth Law: Record-Setting Early Aviator," *National Air and Space Museum*, November 2, 2021, https://airandspace.si.edu/stories/editorial/ruth-law-record-setting-early-aviator.

83 **STINSON QUIT THE POSTAL SERVICE:** Joe Kunzler, "The Life & Times Of Record-Breaking US Aviator Katherine Stinson," *Simple Flying*, July 13, 2022, https://simpleflying.com/katherine-stinson-life-and-times/.

SERIOUSLY CONSIDER . . . WRITING ON HOTEL STATIONERY

84 **IN A 1990 INTERVIEW:** Maya Angelou, "Maya Angelou, The Art of Fiction No. 119," interviewed by George Plimpton, *The Paris Review*, Issue 116, Fall 1990, https://www.theparisreview.org/interviews/2279/the-art-of-fiction-no-119-maya-angelou.

HOW TO BUILD A POSTCARD COLLECTION

88 **MARKETERS FOR THE 1893 COLUMBIAN EXPOSITION:** "Worlds Fairs," *University of Maryland Special Collections*, accessed June 9, 2024, https://exhibitions.lib.umd.edu/postcards/worlds-fairs.

HOW TO WRITE A POSTCARD

91 **A POSTCARD THAT THE WRITER F. SCOTT FITZGERALD:** Sheilah Graham, *The Garden of Allah* (New York: Crown, 1970).

91 **IN 1937, F. SCOTT FITZGERALD TOOK A TRAIN:** Jeffrey Meyers, *Scott Fitzgerald: A Biography* (New York: Harper Perennial, 2014).

91 **RUSSIAN SILENT FILM STAR NAMED ALLA NAZIMOVA:** Gavin Lambert, *Nazimova* (New York: Alfred A. Knopf, 1997).

92 **"HOW ARE YOU? HAVE BEEN MEANING TO COME IN":** F. Scott Fitzgerald to F. Scott Fitzgerald, 193, quoted in Arthur Mizener, "Gatsby, 35 Years Later," *The New York Times*, April 24, 1960.

HOW TO DEVELOP STYLE IN YOUR CORRESPONDENCE

94 **"YOU GOTTA HAVE STYLE":** Diana Vreeland, quoted in Lauren Alexis Fisher, "Diana Vreeland's Most Memorable Quotes," *Harper's Bazaar*, July 29, 2014, https://www.harpersbazaar.com/culture/features/a2964/diana-vreeland-best-quotes/.

94 **"A GARDEN, BUT A GARDEN IN HELL":** Diana Vreeland, quoted in Carol Vogel, "Vreeland's Touches," *The New York Times*, April 1, 1990.

94 **"I CAN'T IMAGINE BECOMING BORED":** Diana Vreeland, quoted in "Red Hots," *WWD*, September 11, 2000, https://wwd.com/fashion-news/fashion-features/article-1199614/.

94 **"EXTRA PIZZAZZ":** Diana Vreeland, quoted in *Diana Vreeland: The Eye Has to Travel*, dirs. Lisa Immordino Vreeland, Bent-Jorgen Perlmutt, and Frédéric Tcheng, 2012, France, Studiocanal. DVD.

95 **"NOBODY IN THEIR RIGHT MIND":** Diana Vreeland, *Diana Vreeland Memos: The Vogue Years*, ed. Alexander Vreeland (New York: Rizzoli, 2015).

96 **"FIGS LOOK HOPEFUL":** Eudora Welty to William Maxwell, 1956, in *What There Is to Say We Have Said: The Correspondence of Eudora Welty and William Maxwell*, ed. Suzanne Marrs (Boston: Mariner Books, 2011). Ebook.

97 **"THE KATHY ACKER THAT YOU WANT":** Kathy Acker email to Mackenzie Wark, in *I'm Very Into You: Correspondence 1995-1996*, ed. Matias Viegener (Cambridge, MA: Semiotext(e), 2015). Reproduced with permission of Semiotext(e).

98 **"OH, MY DEAR FRIEND, MY HEART":** Ernst Lubitsch, dir., *The Shop Around the Corner*, MGM, 1940.

PINK PAPER

104 **"BRIGHT, IMPOSSIBLE":** Elsa Schiaparelli, quoted in Amanda Fortini, "Review: 'Elsa Schiaparelli': Fashion designer too elusive for words," *The Los Angeles Times*, October 30, 2014.

106 **THE BOOK TELLS THE STORY:** Jaqueline Susann. *The Valley of the Dolls* (New York: Grove Press reprint, 2015). Ebook.

106 **ACCORDING TO HER EDITOR:** Michael Korda, "The Rise of Jacqueline Susann," *The New Yorker*, August 5, 1995.

107 **"THE ROUGH RUN THROUGH":** Irving Mansfield, *Life with Jackie* (New York: Bantam Dell, 1983).

107 **"JACKIE, IT SEEMED":** Korda, "Rise of Jacqueline Susann."

108 **"I CAN'T DIE":** Jacqueline Susann, quoted in Barbara Seaman, "Jaqueline Susann," *The Jewish Women's Archive*, accessed June 9, 2024, https://jwa.org/encyclopedia/article/susann-jacqueline.

108 **SIXTY-FIVE CONSECUTIVE WEEKS:** Mia Mercado, "Maybe Don't Take Career Advice from *Valley of the Dolls*," *The Cut*, March 4, 2022.

108 **"JACKIE KNEW HOW TO MANIPULATE":** Bernard Geis, quoted in Amy Fine Collins, "Once Was Never Enough," *Vanity Fair*, January 2000.

HOW TO WRITE ABOUT CLOTHES

116 **"HINTS AND TRICKS AND DREAMS":** Kennedy Fraser, *The Fashionable Mind* (New York: Alfred A. Knopf, 2014). Ebook.

116 **"CLOTHES CAN SUGGEST":** Anne Hollander, *Seeing Through Clothes* (Oakland: University of California Press, 1993).

119 **"LOOKING LIKE A SPANIEL":** Virginia Woolf to Ethel Smyth, 1940, in *The Collected Letters of Virginia Woolf, Vol 6*, eds. Nigel Nicolson and Joanne Trautman (Boston: Mariner Books, 1982).

HOW TO MAINTAIN A GLAMOROUS MYSTIQUE

120 **"TO WALK ALONG BROADWAY":** Maeve Brennan, *The Long-Winded Lady: Notes from The New Yorker* (New York: Counterpoint Press, 2015). Ebook.

121 **"SHE WORE A TIGHT WHITE":** Brennan, *The Long-Winded Lady*. Ebook.

121 **"I KEPT THINKING ABOUT THE GIRL":** Brennan, *The Long-Winded Lady*. Ebook.

122 **SHE BEGAN SLEEPING:** Meghan Racklin, "Maeve Brennan's Unhappy Couples and Disappointed Revolutionaries," *The New Republic*, August 10, 2023.

127 **LEGEND HAS IT THAT LEONARDO:** "The Evolution of the Fountain Pen Through The Ages," *Visconti*, May 8, 2021, https://www.visconti.it/en/magazine/writing/the-evolution-of-the-fountain-pen/.

HOW TO EMBRACE THE PENTERNET

130 **THE** *New York Times*: Isabella Paoletto, "What Killed Penmanship?" *The New York Times*, March 24, 2023.

THE HISTORY OF THE LADIES' PEN

134 **IN MARCH OF 1958:** Jim Mamoulides, "Lady Sheaffer 1958-1964: A Gallery," *PenHero*, January 23, 2023. https://www.penhero.com/PenGallery/Sheaffer/SheafferLadySheaffer1958.htm.

136 **"PATTERNS FOR THE LADY SHEAFFER":** *Sheaffer's Review*, 1958, archived in "Reference Collection: Sheaffer," *Pen Collectors of America*, accessed June 9, 2024, https://pencollectorsofamerica.org/reference-library/sheaffer/.

HOW TO WRITE A LOVE LETTER

137 **"MAXIMS OF DIVINE LOVE":** Heloise to Abelard, in *The Love Letters of Abelard and Heloise*, eds. Israel Gollancz and Honnor Morten (Santa Cruz, CA: Evinity Publishing Inc., 2009). Ebook.

137 **"EVER THINE":** Ludwig van Beethoven, quoted in Alexandra Sifferlin, "Top 10 Famous Love Letters," *Time Magazine*, February 9. 2012, https://newsfeed.time.com/2012/02/14/top-10-famous-love-letters/slide/ludwig-van-beethoven/.

137 **"I WONDER IF YOUR BODY":** Georgia O'Keeffe to Alfred Steiglitz, 1922, in *My Faraway One: Selected Letters of Georgia O'Keeffe and Alfred Stieglitz: Volume One, 1915-1933*, ed. Sarah Greenough (New Haven: Yale University Press, 2011). Ebook.

137 **"GOODNIGHT, MY LITTLE":** James Joyce to Nora Barnacle, 1909, quoted in Nadja Spiegelman, "James Joyce's Love Letters to His "Dirty Little Fuckbird," *The Paris Review*, February 2, 2018, https://www.theparisreview.org/blog/2018/02/02/james-joyces-love-letters-dirty-little-fuckbird/.

137 **"BOSIE":** Oscar Wilde, quoted in *My Own Dear Darling Boy: The Letters of Oscar Wilde to Lord Alfred Douglas*, ed. Ulrich Baer (New York: Warbler Press, 2021). Ebook.

138 **"IF THE FELICITY OF LAST NIGHT":** Mary Wollstonecraft to William Godwin, 1796, quoted in Marc A. Rubenstein, "'My Accursed Origin': The Search for the Mother in *Frankenstein*," *Studies in Romanticism*, 15 (Spring, 1976), 165-94, https://knarf.english.upenn.edu/Articles/rubenst.html.

HOW TO WRITE ABOUT SECRETS

140 *Normal Gossip*: https://www.kelseymckinney.com/normal-gossip.

140 **"GOOD GOSSIP FEELS** *fizzy*": Kelsey McKinney, interviewed for Bear Radio, September 25, 2022.

143 **"MY DEAR ARTHUR":** Oscar Wilde, *Lady Windemere's Fan* (New York: Start Classics, 2014). Ebook.

HOW TO WRITE A BITCHY LETTER

146 **"I AM FORCED TO BE ABUSIVE":** Jane Austen to Cassandra Austen, 1807, in *The Letters of Jane Austen, Brabourne Edition*, ed. Sarah Chauncey Woolsey (Project Gutenberg, February 12, 2013) Ebook.

146 **"WHINNYING OF HARPIES":** E.M. Forster, quoted in "Wickedly Perceptive Words: The Letters of Jane Austen," *Chicago Tribune*, January 7, 1990, https://www.chicagotribune.com/1990/01/07/wickedly-perceptive-words-the-letters-of-jane-austen/.

147 **"OWING TO FRIGHT":** Jane Austen to Cassandra Austen, *Letters of Jane Austen*. Ebook.

148 **WHETHER THE LETTER IS REAL OR NOT:** Tierney Bricker, "Fact Checking *Feud*," *E! News*, March 19, 2017, https://www.eonline.com/news/836544/fact-checking-feud-bette-and-joan-episode-3-the-truth-about-that-kick-to-the-head.

148 **"SHE HAS A CULT":** Joan Crawford, quoted in Kate Figes, *The Big Fat Bitch Book* (New York: Little Brown, 2013). Ebook.

148 **"THERE'S A LOT OF BITCH":** Joan Crawford, quoted in Marissa Oberlander, "Who Killed Joan Crawford? mixes camp and mystery," *Chicago Reader*, October 16, 2019.

HOW TO WRITE A LETTER ABOUT
INTERESTING TIMES

155 **"HOW WONDERFUL TO READ ONCE MORE":** Lillian Ngoyi to Belinda Allan, 1972, in Lilian Ngoyi Papers, Historical Papers Research Archive, University of the Witwatersrand, South Africa. Reproduced with the permission of Nqaba Ngoyi.

156 **"YOU KNOW, I DON'T EVEN WANT TO WRITE LETTERS":** Djuna Barnes to Emily Holmes Colman, 1935, quoted in "History as Literature: The Letters of Djuna Barnes and Emily Holmes Coleman (1935-1936)," ed. G.C. Guirl-Stearley, *The Missouri Review* 22, no. 3 (1999). Reproduced with permission of Authors League Fund and St. Bride's Church, as joint literary executors of the Estate of Djuna Barnes.

157 **"SHE HAS SET UP A SCHEDULE":** Pat Parker to Audre Lorde, in *Sister Love: The Letters of Audre Lorde and Pat Parker 1974-1989*, ed. Julie R. Enzser (Dover, Florida: A Midsummer Night's Press, 2018). Used with permission from the Estate of Pat Parker © 2024 by Anastasia Dunham-Parker-Brady. All rights reserved.

SINCERELY CONSIDER . . . WRITING
AN APOLOGY LETTER

159 **"WHO HAVE MASTERED ETIQUETTE":** Dorothy Parker, "Mrs Post Enlarges on Etiquette," *The New Yorker*, December 23, 1927.

159 **"THE WILLINGNESS TO ACCEPT":** Joan Didion, "Self Respect," *Vogue*, August 1961, 62-63.

A LITTLE NOTE ON . . . WAX SEALS

160 **KATHRYN HASTINGS:** https://kathrynhastingsco.com/.

ON TYPEWRITERS

163 **ROBERT CARO:** Zach Helfand, "Why Robert Caro Now Has Only Ten Typewriters," *The New Yorker*, October 22, 2021.

HOW TO WRITE A LETTER
TO YOUR MOTHER

166 **IN 1975:** Sylvia Plath, *Letters Home: Correspondence 1950-1963*, ed. Aurelia Schober Plath (New York: Harper Perennial, 1992).

166 *Red Comet:* Heather Clark, *Red Comet: The Short Life and Blazing Art of Sylvia Plath* (New York: Alfred A. Knopf, 2020).

166 *Silent Woman:* Janet Malcolm, *The Silent Woman: Sylvia Plath and Ted Hughes* (New York: Vintage, 2013). Ebook.

167 **"PSYCHIC OSMOSIS":** Aurelia Plath, quoted in Maureen Howard, "The Girl Who Tried To Be Good," *The New York Times*, December 14, 1975.

167 **"WOULD HAVE HATED":** Howard, "The Girl Who Tried To Be Good."

167 **"PERCEIVED TO BE PATHOLOGICAL":** Parul Sehgal, "Sylvia Plath's Letters Reveal a Writer Split in Two," *The New York Times*, October 10, 2017.

169 **"THE WRITER AND DIRECTOR NORA EPHRON":** Kristin Marguerite Doidge, *Nora Ephron: A Biography* (Chicago: Chicago Review Press, 2022).

HOW TO WRITE
A LETTER TO YOURSELF

176 **"I SHALL BE A BESTSELLING AUTHOR":** Octavia Butler, Octavia E. Butler papers, the Huntington Library, San Marino, California. Reproduced with permission of Writers House LLC on behalf of the Octavia E. Butler Estate.

177 **"STAY CLEAN":** Stephen King, quoted in *Dear Me: A Letter to My Sixteen-Year-Old Self*, ed. Joseph Galliano (New York: Atria, 2011). Ebook.

177 **"NOTE TO SELF" SEGMENT:** *CBS News*, https://www.cbsnews.com/cbs-mornings/note-to-self/.

177 **"FIND SOME BEAUTIFUL ART":** Maya Angelou, quoted in "Maya Angelou's Note to Self," *CBS News*, September 14, 2013, https://www.cbsnews.com/news/maya-angelous-note-to-self/.

177 **"YOU'LL COME TO APPRECIATE":** Alex Honnold, quoted in "Climber Alex Honnold reflects on what it took to scale a 3,000-foot rock wall with no ropes," *CBS news*, October 9, 2018, https://www.cbsnews.com/news/note-to-self-rock-climber-alex-honnold/.

HOW TO WRITE A LETTER
ABOUT NOTHING AT ALL

180 **"FOOD AND DRINK TO ME":** Henry Miller to Anaïs Nin, 1932, in *A Literate Passion: Letters of Anaïs Nin & Henry Miller: 1932-1953*, ed. Gunther Stuhlmann (Boston: Mariner Books, 1989). Ebook.

180 **"WHY DID THE NOTHING":** James Schuyler to Frank O'Hara, 1955, in *The Letters of James Schuyler to Frank O'Hara*, ed. William Corbett (Brooklyn: Turtle Point Press, 2020). Ebook.

ON STAMPS

182 **AMELIA EARHART WAS A PHILATELIST:** "Noteworthy Stamp Collectors," *Smithsonian National Postal Museum*, accessed January 9, 2024, https://postalmuseum.si.edu/noteworthy-stamp-collectors.

183 **MYSTIC STAMPS:** https://www.mysticstamp.com/.

183 **STUART KATZ STAMPS:** http://stuartkatz.com/.

CONCLUSION

200 **"CORRESPONDENCE IS THE UTOPIAN FORM":** Robert Piglia, *Respiración Artificial* (Barcelona: Debolsillo, 2014). Ebook.

ACKNOWLEDGMENTS

This book exists, first and foremost, because of every single person who answered my impulsive call for pen pals back in 2020 and who put time and energy into navigating a glitchy website meant to coordinate secret Santa exchanges in order to join #PenPalooza and begin sending letters to strangers across the world. I am so grateful to anyone who takes the risk to put pen to paper and seal that paper in an envelope, especially when these actions feel out of step with the rhythms of modern life. But more specifically, this book is dedicated to my longtime correspondents, who keep flinging mail into the ether, against the odds: Megan, Zac, Krupa, Flavia, Alexandra, Caroline, Carolee, Christina, Tracy, Nancy, Debra, Tom, Jenna-Marie, Lauren, Ellie, Kamila, Kristin, Carissa, Sana, Lucy, and so many others that have made my mailbox a place that I look forward to visiting every afternoon. A special thanks to Amy Willen, minha *saudade,* whose letters and surprise packages have bolstered my spirits more times than I can count, and to Rebecca Bact, who is the most beautiful letter-writer I know, and who has reinvigorated the possibilities of the form for me many times over.

This book is also for my husband Erik Hinton, who not only put in tireless hours of research into epistolary history to support this work, but who is, quite literally, my main letter carrier (he has trudged through both rain and snow to drop off my letters in the nearest public mailbox! A trooper!). Whenever I started to think that this book was silly, he would always tell me "Yes, it IS silly, and that's why you have to keep going." Thank you for reminding me that sometimes things should simply be fun. I also want to thank my parents, Joyce and Bill, and my brother, Noah, who all instilled in me a love of the written word, and who comforted me when my summer camp pen pals eventually stopped writing me back.

I am so grateful for the hard work that my editors Sara Neville and Emma Brodie put into the development and creation of this book. Thank you for fighting the good fight and for believing from the beginning that people might want to read about hot glue guns and laminating machines. Thank you also to the team at Clarkson Potter: Angelin Adams, Lise Sukhu, Sahara Clements, Dan Novack, and the countless other hands that have touched this book and made it possible. To my agent, Alia Hanna-Habib: Thank you for being the benevolent genius that you are.

Finally, I want to thank *you,* whoever you are, who reads this book and decides, for the first time in years, to break out your stationery and start writing to someone else. The only way we will continue to perpetuate letter-writing as a literary form is to *do* it, generously and often, and so I am filled with warmth for anyone out there who decides to lick a stamp and take the leap.

Published in the United States by Clarkson Potter/Publishers, an imprint of the Crown Publishing Group, a division of Penguin Random House LLC, New York.
ClarksonPotter.com

CLARKSON POTTER is a trademark and POTTER with colophon is a registered trademark of Penguin Random House LLC.

Library of Congress Cataloging-in-Publication Data is on file with the publisher.

ISBN 978-0-593-23510-2
Ebook ISBN 978-0-593-23511-9

Printed in China

Editor: Sara Neville
Assisting editors: Emma Brodie and Sahara Clements
Designer: Lise Sukhu
Art director: Danielle Deschenes
Production editor: Natalie Blachere
Production manager: Luisa Francavilla
Compositor: Zoe Tokushige
Copyeditor: Diana Drew
Proofreaders: Jacob Sammon and Sasha Tropp
Publicist: David Hawk | Marketer: Chloe Aryeh

Illustrations © by Joana Avillez on pages 76–77, 92, 135, 143, 144–145, 154–155, 164, and 190–191
Snake illustration on pages 146–147 © vinap/Shutterstock.com
Rhinestones and crystrals on page 161 © VitaArtUA/Shutterstock.com and Voltgroup/Shutterstock.com
All other illustrations by Lise Sukhu or sourced from the public domain
Collage artwork by Lise Sukhu

10 9 8 7 6 5 4 3 2 1

First Edition

EAST BRIDGE ON